GAME ON!

Level Up Your Teaching with Gamification

ENGAGE STUDENTS

IMPROVE OUTCOMES

LEVEL UP YOUR TEACHING

JOHN RIGGS

GAME ON!
Level Up Your Teaching with Gamification

Copyright © 2023 by John Riggs

Published by Education Unboxed

ISBN 9798852454263

First Edition

Disclaimers: This book details the author's personal experiences with and opinions on using gamification techniques in education. The author is not liable for any errors, omissions, or actions that result from the application of the information in this book. Any educational activities should be carefully considered in conjunction with school policies and regulations.

Though references and examples of resources are provided, their inclusion does not constitute endorsement. Brand names, logos, and trademarks are used for illustrative purposes only and remain the property of their respective owners.

Introduction

Welcome, fellow educators, to "Game On: Level Up Your Teaching"! Prepare to embark on a journey that will revolutionize your approach to education and transform your classroom into an engaging, dynamic, and student-centered learning environment. Get ready to unlock the power of gamification and witness the incredible impact it can have on your students' enthusiasm, motivation, and academic achievement.

In this book, we will delve into the fascinating realm of gamification, where the principles of game design and mechanics merge with the art of teaching. Together, we will explore how to leverage the innate love for play and competition that resides within all of us to enhance the learning experience and empower our students to reach new heights.

Now, you might be wondering, what exactly is gamification? It's not about turning your classroom into a giant arcade or replacing textbooks with game consoles (though that does sound pretty fun, doesn't it?). Gamification is about harnessing the elements of games - the challenges, rewards, competition, and collaboration - and infusing them into our teaching practices to create an immersive and interactive learning environment.

Imagine a classroom where students are excited to learn, eagerly participating in activities, and taking ownership of their educational journey. Picture students fully engaged, their eyes gleaming with excitement as they conquer academic quests, earn badges, and level up their skills. That's the magic of gamification in action!

Throughout this book, we will uncover the secrets of successful gamification implementation, drawing from real-world examples, research-based strategies, and practical advice. You will discover how to gamify your lessons, design captivating quests and challenges, incorporate game mechanics into your assessments, and foster a positive classroom culture of collaboration and growth.

But let's not forget the most important part – having fun! We'll infuse humor, excitement, and a spirit of adventure into every chapter. After all, teaching should be enjoyable, and learning should be an exhilarating quest. So get ready to unleash your creativity, embrace the unexpected, and take risks as we embark on this gamified teaching adventure together. You'll quickly notice that I end each subchapter with enthusiasm. That's by design – trying new things takes courage, and I'm here to cheer you on! You've got this!

Remember, as educators, we hold the power to shape young minds and ignite the spark of lifelong learning. By embracing the principles of gamification, we can tap into our students' natural curiosity, motivation, and competitive spirit, and transform our classrooms into vibrant hubs of discovery and growth.

So, fellow teachers, let's level up our teaching game and embark on this epic journey of gamification together. Are you ready? It's time to say, "Game On!"

About The Author

Hi, my name is John. I'm a middle school math and literature teacher with over a decade of experience making learning fun and engaging for my students. If you are anything like me, you're always looking for ways to better engage your students and add more zest to your lessons.

Back in 2016 I stumbled onto something called "gamification", before I knew it had a name. My teaching had become routine...aka "boring". I realized that making learning more game-like, with points, levels, challenges, etc. hooked students into the lessons. The students were so much more engaged, motivated, and yes, learning more too!

When I'm not teaching or writing, you can usually find me enjoying time spent with my beautiful and supportive wife, our fun-loving daughters, and our two rambunctious dogs.

"It is the supreme art of the teacher to awaken joy in creative expression and knowledge."

Albert Einstein

CHAPTER ONE

What Is Gamified Learning?

Understanding the Concept of Gamification

In recent years, there has been a growing interest in the concept of utilizing gamelike aspects in education, which is commonly referred to as gamification. As educators, it is of utmost importance for us to delve into this innovative approach and its potential to effectively captivate students in our classrooms. This particular section strives to offer a comprehensive comprehension of gamifying learning and its capacity to inspire students through interactive and immersive learning encounters.

Gamification encompasses the integration of game elements and principles into nongame situations, such as education. By implementing concepts derived from game design, educators possess the capability to convert traditional learning activities into captivating experiences that seize the attention of students. The ultimate objective is to heighten student involvement, motivation, and learning outcomes.

An integral aspect entails the utilization of rewards and incentives, comparable to those encountered in games. Students are acknowledged and rewarded for their accomplishments, progress, and exertion. These rewards can assume various forms, such as points, badges, levels, or virtual currencies, which instill in students a sense of achievement and stimulate their ongoing participation. Furthermore, the introduction of leaderboards and elements of healthy competition can serve as additional sources of motivation for students' engagement.

Another substantial element entails the incorporation of narratives and storytelling. By constructing meaningful and relatable stories, educators can enhance the learning experience, making it more engaging. By placing students in roles which necessitate active participation and problem solving, they develop a sense of ownership regarding their progress and actively involve themselves in the learning process.

Moreover, gamification allows for personalized learning experiences. Through the utilization of adaptive learning platforms or game based learning applications, students can receive tailored content and challenges that align with their individual strengths, weaknesses, and progress. This customized approach not only cultivates a deeper understanding among students but also fosters a sense of autonomy and self-directed learning.

It is crucial to note that I am not proposing the replacement of traditional teaching methods with gamified learning, but rather the enhancement of these methods. Gamified learning can be seamlessly integrated into existing curricula and instructional strategies. By amalgamating gamification with other teaching approaches, educators can establish a dynamic and captivating learning environment that caters to various learning styles and preferences.

Comprehending gamification holds significant importance for educators striving to enhance student engagement and motivation. By incorporating game elements, rewards, narratives, and personalized learning experiences, gamified learning possesses the potential to revolutionize conventional classrooms into interactive and effective learning spaces. Embracing gamification in education permits us to tap into the inherent motivation and enthusiasm of students, thus nurturing a genuine passion for learning that extends beyond the confines of the classroom.

Benefits of Gamified Learning in the Classroom

"The incorporation of gamification into the realm of education has attracted considerable attention as an inventive means to captivate and enrich students' learning experiences. This section delves into the advantages of integrating gamification into the classroom, addressing the needs of teachers seeking to adopt this approach in their teaching methods.

One of the primary merits of gamification in education lies in its capacity to heighten student motivation and engagement. By harnessing students' inherent inclination towards games, educators can cultivate an interactive and dynamic learning environment that captures their attention and actively involves them in the learning process. This heightened engagement leads to increased participation, better retention of information, and an augmented enthusiasm for learning.

Furthermore, gamified learning nurtures a sense of autonomy and self directed learning. By incorporating game elements such as quests, challenges, and rewards, students are empowered to take control of their learning journey. They are endowed with the liberty to chart their own paths, set goals, and make decisions, thereby fostering a sense of responsibility and independence. This intrinsic motivation propels students to explore and unravel knowledge on their own, facilitating a deeper understanding of the subject matter.

In addition, gamification fosters collaboration and teamwork among students. Many gamified learning platforms offer opportunities for students to collaborate, working together to solve problems and achieve shared objectives. By cultivating a cooperative atmosphere, students develop critical skills such as communication, negotiation, and cooperation, all of which are indispensable for success in the contemporary world.

Moreover, gamified learning provides students with immediate feedback, enabling them to track their progress and adapt accordingly. Through interactive features like leaderboards, badges, and levels, students can effortlessly evaluate their performance and identify areas that require improvement. This instantaneous feedback not only motivates students but also instills a growth mindset and a willingness to take risks.

Lastly, gamification has the potential to render complex concepts more accessible and enjoyable. By presenting information in a gamified format, abstract ideas can be transformed into interactive and relatable experiences. This approach caters to diverse learning styles and encourages a profound comprehension of the subject matter.

As can be observed, gamified learning yields numerous advantages for educators endeavoring to cultivate an interactive and dynamic learning environment for their students. By harnessing the power of gamification, educators can bolster student motivation, foster autonomy and collaboration, provide timely feedback, and create an enjoyable learning experience. The integration of gamified learning in the classroom possesses the potential to revolutionize education and equip students for success in the contemporary world.

Implementation: Challenges and Concerns

Educators are actively exploring novel approaches to captivate their students. By integrating game aspects into the classroom setting, teachers can tap into the innate motivation and pleasure derived from playing games. However, there exist numerous challenges and considerations linked to the implementation of gamification that educators should be mindful of.

One primary challenge pertains to the substantial time and effort demanded for the planning and development process. Designing a gamified curriculum requires the creation of a framework, the establishment of goals, and the mapping out of specific game elements to be utilized. Teachers must also navigate through the technical aspects, which entail selecting suitable digital tools or platforms to facilitate the gamified experience. Given the already arduous workload, this process can be time consuming and demanding.

Another concern involves ensuring the alignment of gamified learning with the curriculum and learning objectives. While the integration of game elements can enhance engagement, it is imperative to find a balance between entertainment and educational content. Teachers must guarantee that the game elements contribute to the learning experience rather than divert attention from it. This necessitates meticulous planning and continuous evaluation to ensure that the gamified activities are in line with the desired learning outcomes.

Acquiring student buy-in poses yet another challenge that teachers may encounter when introducing gamification. Some students may resist or dismiss gamified learning as "childish" or not academically rigorous enough. It is vital for educators to address these concerns and emphasize the educational benefits. By effectively communicating the purpose and relevance of gamified learning, teachers can assist students in recognizing its value and fostering their active participation.

Furthermore, the integration of technology can be intimidating for teachers who may lack familiarity or comfort with digital tools. Teachers require sufficient training and support to effectively utilize the necessary technology. This includes troubleshooting any technical issues that may arise during the implementation process.

While the gamification of learning holds promise for engaging students, it is crucial for teachers to acknowledge and address the associated challenges. These challenges encompass the time and effort required for planning and development, ensuring alignment with the curriculum and learning objectives, gaining student buyin, and effectively integrating technology. By proactively tackling these challenges, teachers can leverage the power of gamified learning to create a dynamic and captivating classroom environment.

CHAPTER TWO

Getting Started with Gamification

Setting Clear Learning Objectives

When it comes to gamified learning, one thing we can't overlook is the importance of clear and actionable learning objectives. As educators, it's crucial for us to establish precise goals that provide both students and ourselves with guidance throughout the learning process. In this section, we'll dive into why clear learning objectives are so significant in the context of gamification, and we'll also share some practical strategies to engage students and enrich their learning experience.

Now, gamification of learning is all about infusing game elements into the classroom to spark active participation, intrinsic motivation, and that satisfying sense of accomplishment. But here's the thing: without clear learning objectives, those game elements can easily turn into distractions that hinder students' progress. By setting clear objectives, teachers can ensure that game mechanics align with educational goals, so that every element of the game contributes to student learning.

Let's start with how clear learning objectives benefit students. These objectives act as a roadmap for their learning journey. When objectives are spelled out clearly, students know exactly what's expected of them and can keep track of their progress. This clarity empowers them to take ownership of their learning, fostering a sense of agency and self-directedness.

But it's not just students who benefit from clear learning objectives; teachers do too. These objectives serve as a compass, guiding teachers in designing gamified activities that align with specific learning outcomes. Teachers can identify the game mechanics and elements that best support the achievement of these objectives, creating meaningful engagement and enhancing student learning.

To establish clear learning objectives, we need to consider the specific content and skills that we want to address. We should aim for objectives that are specific, measurable, attainable, relevant, and time-bound (yes, they're SMART!). This framework ensures that our objectives are realistic and achievable, while also challenging students to grow.

Now, it's not enough to have SMART objectives; we also need to effectively communicate them to our students. Clearly articulating the learning objectives at the beginning of a gamified unit or lesson gives students a clear sense of purpose and direction. We can use visual aids like charts or posters to prominently display the objectives in the classroom, serving as constant reminders that motivate students to strive for their goals.

Ultimately, clear learning objectives are the foundation of gamified learning. By defining specific goals, teachers can align game elements with educational outcomes, enabling students to embrace purpose and direction. Clear objectives empower students to take charge of their learning, while also guiding teachers in designing engaging and effective gamified activities. By thoughtfully integrating game mechanics, teachers can create an immersive and transformative learning experience for students.

Remember, gamified learning is like adding a sprinkle of magic to education. Embrace the power of clear learning objectives and embark on an exciting journey of gamified learning!

Choosing the Right Game Elements for Your Classroom

Education can be a bit of a maze, but thankfully, gamification has emerged as a fantastic strategy to captivate students and make learning a whole lot more exciting. By infusing game elements into the classroom, teachers can create an interactive environment that gets students actively involved. But here's the secret sauce: you need to carefully choose the right game elements that align with your teaching goals and objectives.

Step one on this gamification journey is figuring out what you want your students to achieve. Are you aiming to boost their critical thinking, encourage collaboration, or unleash their inner creativity? Once you've got a clear picture of your objectives, it's time to pick the game elements that will help you achieve those goals.

One nifty game element you can introduce is points and rewards. By assigning points for completing tasks or mastering concepts, you're giving your students a little taste of the sweet nectar of motivation. And hey, those points can be cashed in for rewards like privileges or good old-fashioned recognition. Not only does this get them actively participating, but it also reinforces positive behavior and the effort they put in.

Next up on the game element menu is good old competition. Injecting some friendly rivalry into the classroom can really spice things up. Leaderboards displaying students' progress and achievements can create a buzz of excitement and engagement. You see, humans have this innate drive to outshine their peers, so competition can inspire your students to go that extra mile and achieve academic greatness.

Collaboration is a game element that shouldn't be overlooked. By throwing in some group activities or team-based challenges, you're giving your students the chance to work together, communicate like pros, and sharpen their problem-solving skills. It's like building a tight-knit squad in the classroom, fostering a sense of camaraderie and creating a supportive community.

Oh, and let's not forget about personalization. Each student is a unique individual with their own set of strengths and interests. By letting them choose their learning path or customize their avatars, you're handing them the reins and letting them take control of their own learning adventure. Talk about empowerment!

Brace yourself, because when you implement gamification in the classroom, magical things can happen. But remember, you've got to choose the right game elements that align with your teaching goals. Mix it up with a winning combination of points and rewards, healthy competition, collaboration, and personalization, and you'll create a learning environment that's not only interactive and immersive but also super engaging and set for academic success.

Now, go forth and gamify like a boss!

Creating a Game-Based Curriculum

Let's dive into the exciting realm of creating a curriculum that brings the magic of games into the classroom! In this section, we'll explore practical strategies and insights for all you teachers out there who are eager to embark on the journey of gamified learning.

The first step in developing a game-based curriculum is to establish clear learning objectives. We want to make sure that game mechanics and content align with our educational goals, so the game becomes an effective instructional tool instead of a mere distraction. This means pinpointing the essential concepts and skills that our students need to master and designing game elements that reinforce and assess these learning outcomes.

Once we've got our objectives in place, it's time to select the right game mechanics and structures that support those goals. We can consider elements like points, levels, badges, and leaderboards to create a sense of healthy competition and achievement. It's also important to strike a balance between individual and collaborative gameplay and integrate feedback and assessment mechanisms that promote continuous improvement.

Creating a game-based curriculum requires some serious planning and design skills. We need to carefully plan the progression of challenges, making sure they become progressively more complex and scaffolded to support student growth. And hey, let's not forget about the game's narrative and theme! These elements can really amp up student engagement and immerse them in the learning process.

Implementing a game-based curriculum calls for a supportive classroom environment. We need to clearly communicate expectations and rules while also giving our students a sense of autonomy and agency within the game. This helps cultivate a positive and collaborative culture where students feel motivated and empowered to take charge of their own learning. It's all about creating that perfect blend of structure and freedom.

Last but not least, ongoing assessment and reflection are essential parts of a game-based curriculum. We need to regularly evaluate how effective our game elements are in achieving the desired learning outcomes. And guess what? Feedback from our students is gold! By gathering their input and adapting the game as needed, we keep it dynamic and relevant, ensuring it remains a powerful learning tool.

So, my fellow educators, let's embrace the power of gamification in learning! By tapping into the intrinsic motivation and engagement that games offer, we can transform our classrooms into interactive and immersive learning experiences. This journey will ultimately foster deeper understanding and long-lasting retention of key concepts and skills.

Are you ready to level up? Let the gamified learning adventure begin!

CHAPTER THREE

Designing Engaging Game-Based Lessons

Incorporating Gamified Elements in Lesson Planning

Let's dive into the exciting world of incorporating gamified elements into our lesson planning! As educators, we're always on the lookout for innovative teaching methods that can truly captivate and motivate our students. In this section, we'll explore how we can infuse our lesson plans with game-inspired elements to create an interactive and immersive learning environment that boosts student engagement and motivation.

One strategy that works like a charm is introducing rewards and incentives inspired by games. You know, those points, badges, and levels that students can earn as they make progress in their learning. These rewards not only acknowledge their achievements but also give them a delightful sense of fulfillment, inspiring them to keep pushing forward on their educational journey.

Another approach is to spice things up with challenges or quests that resemble games. By framing your learning objectives as exciting missions, you're making the content more relatable and enjoyable for your students. Imagine them stepping into the shoes of detectives, unraveling historical mysteries by examining evidence and making connections. Talk about an adventure!

But we can't forget the power of interactive technology tools. We can leverage online platforms that offer interactive quizzes or educational games, seamlessly integrating them into our lesson plans. These tools not only encourage active participation but also reinforce our learning objectives. Students can learn at their own pace, receiving immediate feedback that boosts their comprehension and retention of the material. It's like turning learning into a thrilling game!

Now, it's important to remember that gamification should never overshadow substantive learning. It's a tool that enhances the learning process, not replaces it. That's why it's crucial to align our gamified elements with our curriculum objectives and learning outcomes. We're creating a harmonious blend of fun and educational goodness.

Incorporating gamified elements into our lesson planning calls for creativity, adaptability, and a willingness to experiment. It's about embracing a fresh approach that transforms our classrooms into engaging and dynamic environments, where the flame of passion for learning burns bright. So, let's seize the potential of gamified learning as educators and embark on a journey that revolutionizes education, empowering our students to unleash their full potential.

Get ready for an adventure like no other! Game on!

Strategies for Effective Game-Based Instruction

Let's dive into the exciting world of game-based instruction, where education meets fun! In today's modern era, incorporating game elements in teaching has become a captivating and innovative method. By infusing our lessons with game-like aspects, we can truly engage our students and take their learning experiences to a whole new level. In this section, we'll explore some practical strategies that will help us make the most of this approach.

First things first, we need to establish clear learning objectives. Before we dive into the games, let's make sure that the content and mechanics align perfectly with our curriculum standards. We want to create meaningful learning experiences that hit the nail on the head.

When selecting games, choose ones that are suitable for your subject matter and the age group of your students. Look for games that offer educational value, promote critical thinking, and provide opportunities for collaboration and problem-solving. It's all about finding the right game for the right lesson.

Now, it's important to support our students throughout their game-based journey. Before jumping into the gameplay, offer them the necessary background knowledge and skills to succeed. Provide pre-game activities, tutorials, or brief lessons to prepare them and ensure they grasp the concepts we're teaching.

Reflection and feedback are key players in this game. Encourage your students to reflect on their gameplay experiences and connect them to the learning objectives. Offer constructive feedback to guide their progress and help them grow.

Teamwork makes the dream work! Games can be fantastic tools for promoting collaboration. Incorporate cooperative gameplay or group challenges that require students to work together, solve problems, make decisions, and achieve shared goals. It's all about fostering that team spirit.

Don't forget the power of gamification mechanics! Alongside the games themselves, utilize mechanics like points, badges, leaderboards, and level progression. These little tricks motivate and engage students, providing instant feedback, healthy competition, and a satisfying sense of achievement.

Balance is key! Find that sweet spot between challenge and enjoyment in the games you choose. Make sure the difficulty level suits your students, offering them a sense of accomplishment when they conquer obstacles, all while keeping the gameplay engaging and enjoyable.

Assess, assess, assess! Integrate both formative and summative assessments throughout your game-based instruction. Use quizzes, discussions, or written reflections to evaluate your students' understanding and progress. It's all about checking in and providing the guidance they need.

By implementing these strategies, we can tap into the true potential of gamification and create a stimulating and effective learning environment. Game-based instruction motivates our students, enhances their critical thinking skills, promotes collaboration, and helps them develop a deep understanding of the subject matter. So let's embrace this approach and revolutionize education, equipping our students with the skills they need to conquer the digital world of the 21st century.

Ready to play and learn? Let the games begin!

Adapting Traditional Lessons into Gamified Activities

Education is constantly evolving, and it's crucial for us teachers to find creative methods that capture our students' attention and contribute to their success. One approach that's gaining popularity is gamified learning. It's all about harnessing the power of games to take the learning experience to a whole new level. In this section, we'll dive into the concept of adapting traditional lessons into gamified activities, giving you some practical strategies to sprinkle some gamification magic in your classroom.

Traditional lessons can sometimes feel a bit, well, linear. Students passively absorb information from textbooks and lectures, and it's easy for their attention to drift away. But fear not! Gamified learning is here to save the day. By transforming your lessons into gamified activities, you'll create an engaging and interactive experience that grabs your students' attention and motivates them to actively participate.

The first step in this gamification journey is identifying your core learning objectives. We don't want to just slap on some game elements and call it a day. No, no. Gamification should go hand in hand with educational content. By aligning game mechanics with specific learning outcomes, you'll ensure that your students not only have a blast but also develop a deep understanding of the subject matter.

Now, let's talk about game elements. Points, levels, and achievements, oh my! These can be game-changers in tracking your students' progress and giving them a satisfying sense of accomplishment. Imagine turning a history lesson into a thrilling trivia game, where students earn points for correct answers and unlock new levels as they advance. It's excitement and healthy competition rolled into one.

Get ready to unleash your storytelling prowess. By weaving a compelling narrative into your lessons, you'll create an emotional connection that makes the learning experience more memorable. Picture a science lesson on the solar system transforming into an interactive adventure, where students explore planets, solve puzzles, and work together to save the galaxy. It's like stepping into their very own sci-fi movie!

To ensure the success of your gamified activities, clear instructions and a supportive learning environment are key. Communicate the rules and objectives of the game with crystal clarity, and provide continuous feedback and guidance to your students. Remember to embrace flexibility and adaptability, as students may progress at different paces. We're all in this game together!

Adapting traditional lessons into gamified activities is a surefire way to engage your students and elevate their learning experiences. By incorporating game elements, storytelling, and clear objectives, you'll create a dynamic and interactive classroom environment that ignites curiosity, motivation, and deep understanding. Embracing gamification is like giving education a turbo boost, equipping your students with the skills they need to conquer the 21st century with confidence.

Let's level up our teaching game and make learning an epic adventure!

CHAPTER FOUR

Utilizing Technology in Gamified Learning

Selecting Appropriate Digital Tools for Gamified Learning

In the vast landscape of digital tools and platforms available today, choosing the right ones for gamification can seem like navigating a maze. This subchapter will guide you through the process of selecting the perfect digital tools that will elevate your gamified learning experience to new heights!

Define Your Objectives

Before diving headfirst into the sea of options, take a moment to clarify your goals and objectives. What specific learning outcomes do you want to achieve through gamification? Do you want to improve collaboration, reinforce content knowledge, or enhance critical thinking skills? Having a clear understanding of your objectives will help you make informed decisions when selecting digital tools.

Consider Student Preferences

Remember, the heart and soul of gamification are the students themselves. Take into account their preferences, interests, and technological capabilities. Are they more inclined towards competitive games or collaborative activities? Are they comfortable using specific devices or platforms? By considering student preferences, you'll ensure that the digital tools you choose resonate with them and spark their enthusiasm.

Research, Research, Research

Once you have a solid grasp of your objectives and student preferences, it's time to dive into the realm of research. Explore different websites, platforms, and apps that align with your goals. Read reviews, seek recommendations from fellow educators, and even test out the tools yourself. Remember, knowledge is power, and the more you know about a digital tool, the better equipped you'll be to make an informed decision.

Seek Compatibility

As you explore various digital tools, consider their compatibility with your existing classroom infrastructure. Will the tool integrate smoothly with your learning management system or other educational platforms you use? Does it require additional devices or software? Ensuring compatibility will save you from potential headaches and allow for a seamless integration of gamification into your classroom.

Trial and Error

Just like in the world of gaming, trial and error is key. Don't be afraid to experiment with different digital tools and platforms. Start with a small pilot project or use a tool for a specific activity to gauge its effectiveness. Pay attention to student feedback and adjust accordingly. Remember, it's all part of the learning process, and through trial and error, you'll discover the digital tools that work best for you and your students.

Embrace the Power of Community

The beauty of being an educator in the digital age is the wealth of knowledge and support available within the education community. Connect with fellow teachers, attend professional development workshops, or join online communities dedicated to gamification. By tapping into the collective wisdom and experiences of others, you'll uncover hidden gems and receive valuable insights on selecting the right digital tools.

In the end, selecting appropriate digital tools for gamification is a journey of exploration and discovery. By defining your objectives, considering student preferences, conducting thorough research, seeking compatibility, embracing trial and error, and leveraging the power of community, you'll embark on a path that leads to gamified learning experiences that truly engage and inspire your students. So, gear up, my fellow gamification enthusiasts, and let the quest for the perfect digital tools begin!

Integrating Gamification with Learning Management Systems

Let's dive into the exciting world of integrating gamification with learning management systems (LMS)! Gamification is all about bringing game elements and mechanics into non-game contexts to boost learner engagement and motivation. And you know what? LMS platforms like Google Classroom and others are the perfect playgrounds for this adventure. They're widely used by teachers for content delivery and student progress tracking. So, let's explore some practical ways to seamlessly incorporate gamification into LMS platforms and transform how students interact with educational content.

One key aspect of gamification in LMS is the implementation of badges, points, and leaderboards. Think of it as giving your students virtual medals, points, and a stage to show off their achievements. Awarding badges for task completion or reaching learning milestones taps into their desire for recognition and achievement. And hey, let's assign points for correct answers or timely assignment submissions to motivate active participation and excellence. It's like turning learning into a thrilling game show! Oh, and don't forget about leaderboards. They add that extra spice of healthy competition as students aim for the top positions. Who doesn't love a little friendly rivalry?

Get ready for quests and missions. Forget about those traditional assignments and quizzes. We're talking about designing quests that require students to embark on a series of exciting tasks and challenges. By framing learning objectives as quests, you're immersing your students in an epic learning adventure. It's like unleashing their inner heroes! And guess what? Successful quest completion can unlock additional content or rewards, making their journey even more thrilling. Talk about motivation boosters!

Let's not overlook the power of storytelling. You know how stories capture our imaginations and transport us to different worlds? Well, teachers can create narratives or scenarios that contextualize the learning material, turning it into a captivating adventure. By immersing students in a storyline, you make learning more relatable and memorable. It's like giving education a plot twist that leaves a lasting impact. Better comprehension and retention? Check!

Integrating gamification with learning management systems opens up incredible opportunities for teachers to engage and motivate their students. By incorporating badges, points, leaderboards, quests, and storytelling, LMS platforms can evolve into immersive learning environments that capture students' attention and ignite a true passion for learning. So, let's harness the power of gamification, revolutionize content delivery, and create an enjoyable learning experience that leads to improved academic outcomes.

Ready to level up your teaching game? Let's dive into the world of gamified learning with our LMS platforms and make education an epic adventure!

Assessing Student Progress with Gamified Technology

In today's digital era, technology has become an integral part of our lives, and education is no exception. As teachers, it's crucial for us to adapt to the ever-changing educational landscape and embrace innovative methods that truly engage and motivate our students, leading to improved learning outcomes.

One approach that has gained popularity is gamified learning, which harnesses the power of games to foster intrinsic motivation, collaboration, and critical thinking skills among students. However, as educators, we need to recognize the importance of assessing student progress within this new learning environment. Luckily, gamified technology offers a wide range of assessment tools and strategies that can help us effectively evaluate student learning.

One of the great advantages of gamified technology is its ability to provide real-time feedback to both students and teachers. Through interactive quizzes, simulations, and game-based assignments, students receive immediate feedback on their performance, enabling them to identify their strengths and areas that need improvement. As teachers, we can use this feedback to tailor our instruction and provide targeted support to students who may benefit from it the most.

Another benefit of gamified technology is its capacity to track and analyze student data. By using learning management systems and game-based platforms, we can gather valuable insights into student progress, such as time spent on tasks, levels completed, and mastery of specific concepts. This data informs our instructional decisions, allowing us to design personalized learning paths for our students and effectively address their individual needs.

Furthermore, gamified technology empowers us to create authentic and engaging assessments that go beyond traditional paper-and-pencil tests. We can design quests, challenges, and simulations that require students to apply their knowledge and skills in real-world contexts. These assessments not only evaluate students' understanding but also cultivate higher-order thinking skills, problem-solving abilities, and creativity.

However, it's important to remember that while gamified technology offers valuable assessment opportunities, it shouldn't replace the formative and summative assessments we already use. Instead, it should be seen as a complementary tool that enhances our existing assessment practices.

Assessing student progress within the gamified learning environment is essential to ensure effective learning outcomes. Gamified technology provides diverse assessment tools and strategies that offer real-time feedback, track student data, and facilitate authentic assessments. By harnessing these tools, we can create a dynamic and engaging learning experience for our students, enhancing their motivation, collaboration, and critical thinking skills. As teachers, it's imperative that we embrace gamified technology and harness its potential to assess student progress effectively, ultimately promoting meaningful learning experiences.

CHAPTER FIVE

Fostering Collaboration and Competition in the Classroom

Promoting Cooperative Learning through Gamification

Let's dive into the exciting world of promoting cooperative learning through gamification! Cooperative learning has long been recognized for its ability to boost student engagement, critical thinking skills, and academic performance. It creates a positive classroom environment that fosters collaboration, communication, and problem-solving. But hey, we all know implementing cooperative learning strategies can be a bit challenging, especially in schools. That's where gamification comes in, stealing the spotlight for good reason. It has the power to turn traditional learning experiences into immersive and interactive adventures. By integrating gamified elements into cooperative learning activities, teachers can cultivate an environment that ignites students' motivation to work together, learn from one another, and achieve shared objectives.

One effective approach to promote cooperative learning is by introducing team-based challenges and quests. These activities are designed to encourage collaboration, communication, and knowledge-sharing among students within their teams. By setting clear objectives, offering meaningful rewards, and fostering a healthy sense of competition, teachers can create an atmosphere of excitement and engagement in the classroom. It's like turning learning into an epic quest where students join forces to conquer challenges!

Another strategy is to utilize gamified assessment tools that allow students to demonstrate their understanding of the material while working cooperatively. Picture this: online quizzes with leaderboard features or interactive puzzles that require teamwork to solve. By incorporating elements of competition and cooperation, these assessments not only motivate students to actively participate but also provide opportunities for peer learning and support. Learning becomes a team sport!

Furthermore, gamification can be a game-changer in establishing a sense of achievement and progress within cooperative learning experiences. Implementing a leveling system or a point-based reward system enables students to track their individual and team progress. It's like unlocking new levels in a video game! This not only encourages healthy competition but also instills a sense of responsibility and accountability among students to contribute to their team's success.

When done right, gamification serves as a powerful tool to promote and sustain cooperative learning in classrooms. By incorporating game elements and mechanics into cooperative learning activities, teachers create an engaging and motivating environment where students collaborate, communicate, and learn from one another. From team-based challenges and quests to gamified assessment tools, the possibilities are endless. So, let's embrace the magic of gamification in learning and witness the thriving of our students! Together, we can make cooperative learning an epic adventure!

Implementing Team-Based Challenges and Quests

In the exciting world of education, it's crucial to find innovative and captivating approaches to ignite students' curiosity and foster a genuine passion for learning. By infusing the classroom with game elements, educators can create an immersive and interactive environment that sparks students' active engagement in their educational journey.

One powerful method for implementing gamified learning is the introduction of team-based challenges and quests. These activities not only promote collaboration and teamwork but also provide students with an opportunity to apply their knowledge and skills in practical and meaningful ways.

Team-based challenges and quests can take many forms, ranging from solving intricate puzzles and riddles to completing real-life simulations and projects. By dividing students into teams, educators foster a healthy spirit of competition that motivates students to collaborate, share ideas, and support each other in achieving a common goal.

These challenges can be thoughtfully designed to align with specific learning goals and curriculum standards, ensuring that students derive both enjoyment and essential knowledge and skills. For example, in a history class, students might embark on a quest to research and present a comprehensive timeline of significant events. In a science class, they could take on a challenge that requires designing and constructing a functional model to demonstrate a scientific principle.

To ensure the success of team-based challenges and quests, it's essential to provide clear instructions, establish transparent criteria for success, and set realistic goals. Educators should also actively monitor and provide feedback to the teams throughout the process, encouraging reflection and continuous improvement.

Furthermore, creating a supportive and inclusive environment where every student feels valued and included is paramount. Team-based challenges and quests offer an excellent opportunity to foster a sense of belonging as students learn to appreciate and leverage the unique strengths and perspectives of their teammates.

The incorporation of team-based challenges and quests represents a powerful approach to engage students through the magic of gamified learning. By integrating game-like elements into the classroom, educators can cultivate an environment that nurtures collaboration, critical thinking, problem-solving, and creativity. These activities not only make the learning experience more enjoyable but also equip students with essential skills for success in the 21st century. So, let the adventures begin, and get ready to witness your students thrive!

Harnessing the Power of Competition to Enhance Learning

Competition has always been a wild beast that can light up the fire of motivation in various aspects of life, and education is no exception. When it comes to gamified learning, competition takes on a whole new level of awesomeness. By infusing the learning process with competitive elements, educators can create an environment that ignites active participation, collaboration, and an insatiable hunger for improvement.

One of the best things about competition in gamified learning is its ability to tap into students' innate craving for challenge and achievement. When students are presented with clear goals to conquer, like earning points, badges, or leveling up, their desire to conquer those challenges goes through the roof. This inner motivation becomes a turbo boost that propels them to put in more effort and conquer any obstacles in their way.

Competition also fuels collaboration among students. By forming teams or setting up leaderboards, educators can foster peer-to-peer interaction and teamwork. Students get to join forces, brainstorm ideas, and support each other's learning journeys. This not only amplifies their understanding of the subject matter but also hones their superpowers of social skills and the ability to work as part of an unstoppable team.

And here's the cherry on top: competition serves up instant feedback to students on their progress and performance. With real-time scoring or ranking systems, students can gauge their own superhero abilities and compare them with those of their classmates. This feedback loop gives them the power to identify their strengths and weaknesses, making it possible to swoop in with targeted action to level up their skills.

To make the most of competition in gamified learning, educators need to strike the perfect balance. While a healthy dose of competition can spark student engagement like lightning bolts, going overboard and obsessing about winning can turn the fun into stress and anxiety. So, it's crucial to create a supportive and inclusive learning universe where every student feels like a superhero, empowered and motivated to conquer any challenge that comes their way.

Competition is a superpower in the realm of gamified learning, capable of unleashing student engagement and motivation like a lightning storm. By incorporating elements of competition, such as points, badges, and leaderboards, educators can tap into students' natural hunger for challenge and achievement. Competition fuels collaboration, dishes out immediate feedback, and shapes essential social skills. But remember, balance is key. Creating a supportive learning space where all students can unleash their inner superheroes is what truly makes gamified learning a mind-blowing experience. So, let the games begin and watch your students rise to the occasion, ready to conquer the challenges of the real world with gusto!

CHAPTER SIX

Assessing and Evaluating Gamified Learning

The Art of Assessing:
Formative and Summative Strategies

Assessment is the secret sauce that spices up the learning process. It gives teachers the power to gauge student progress, pinpoint areas for improvement, and dish out timely feedback. When it comes to gamifying lessons, assessment becomes even more crucial. It helps us measure the impact of gamification on student engagement and achievement. So, let's dive into the world of assessment strategies, both ongoing and final, that can take our gamified learning to the next level.

First up, we have formative assessment, the cool cousin of assessments. It's all about gathering continuous feedback along the learning journey. Within the world of gamified learning, formative assessment seamlessly blends with gameplay. Think in-game quizzes, puzzles, or challenges that slyly assess students' understanding of the content. These assessments can even adapt to each student's performance, delivering personalized feedback and guidance. Talk about a tailor-made learning experience!

Now, let's talk about badges and achievements—the superheroes of formative assessment. As students power through the game, they earn badges and unlock achievements based on their mastery of skills and knowledge. These badges not only boost motivation but also serve as shiny proof of progress. By checking out the badges earned by each student, teachers get a glimpse into their strengths and areas for growth. It's like collecting superpowers!

Moving on to the grand finale, we have summative assessment, the ultimate showdown. This happens at the end of a unit or course to evaluate overall mastery. In the world of gamified learning, summative assessment gets a makeover. Picture a final challenge that students conquer or a culmination of epic tasks that showcase their learning. It's not just an assessment, it's a thrilling adventure where students can shine and celebrate their achievements.

And there's one more trick up our sleeves—portfolios! Students can create digital portfolios that showcase their gamified learning journey. These portfolios become a treasure trove of achievements, reflections, and evidence of growth. Sharing these portfolios with teachers and peers creates a full-circle view of students' progress and growth. It's like showcasing their skills on a virtual red carpet!

Formative and summative assessment strategies are the secret weapons of gamified learning. By seamlessly blending assessments into gameplay and unleashing the power of badges, achievements, quizzes, and portfolios, teachers can measure student progress, deliver timely feedback, and evaluate the success of gamified learning. It's a dynamic and engaging learning environment where students are motivated, collaborate, and achieve greatness. So, let's rock these assessments and make gamified learning a legendary adventure!

Unveiling the Secrets of Student Progress: Tracking and Analyzing Like a Pro

In the exciting realm of gamified learning, keeping tabs on student progress is like having a secret superpower. As educators, understanding how our students are doing is crucial for delivering effective instruction and personalizing their learning experience. So, let's dive into the world of tracking and evaluating student progress within a gamified learning environment and discover the tools and methods that make it all possible.

One nifty approach to track student progress is through the power of data analysis. By collecting and analyzing data on student performance, we unlock valuable insights into their strengths and weaknesses. This insight empowers us to tailor our instruction and support to meet their individual needs. Gamified learning platforms often come equipped with built-in analytics tools that give us the lowdown on student progress, from completion rates and scores to time spent on different tasks or levels. It's like having a treasure map to guide us to areas where students may need some extra help.

But that's not all! We also have the magical world of digital badges and achievements. In the gamified learning kingdom, students earn badges and achievements as they conquer challenges and make progress. These badges become visual representations of their mastery in various skills and knowledge areas. Best of all, they serve as little beacons of motivation, guiding students forward on their learning journey. And for us, educators, they become powerful tracking tools that allow us to see just how far our students have come.

Gamified learning platforms often offer features that provide real-time feedback and assessment. Through interactive quizzes, mini-games, and simulations, students get instant feedback on their performance. It's like having a personal coach cheering them on and guiding their next moves. And for us, educators, this real-time feedback is pure gold. It helps us spot any misconceptions or gaps in understanding and intervene with lightning speed.

And here's the grand finale: tracking and analyzing student progress can reveal fascinating trends and patterns in the learning process. By diving into the data on student engagement, participation, and performance, we unlock the secrets of what works best for our students in the gamified learning realm. Armed with this knowledge, we can make informed instructional decisions and continuously improve our gamified learning environment. It's like being a detective, solving the mystery of how to create the most engaging and effective learning experience.

Tracking and analyzing student progress are the secret weapons of gamified learning. With data analytics, digital badges, real-time feedback, and assessment tools in our arsenal, we gain valuable insights into student performance and can tailor our instruction to their unique needs. It's like crafting a personalized adventure for each student, guiding them towards success. So, let's embrace the power of tracking and analysis in gamified learning and unlock a world of personalized, engaging, and transformative education!

Unleashing the Power of Gamified Learning: Assessing Its Impact

Ah, gamified learning, the cool kid on the education block, bringing a whole new level of engagement and interactivity to the classroom. But hey, let's not just ride the trend wave without understanding its true impact and the amazing benefits it brings to the table. In this section, we're diving deep into the world of gamified learning to uncover its effects and explore how it's revolutionizing education.

Now, when it comes to assessing the effectiveness of gamified learning, we've got some key factors to consider. First off, gamified learning puts students in the driver's seat, giving them a sense of autonomy and control over their own learning experience. With progress tracking, achievement badges, and leveling up, students become the heroes of their own learning journey. And guess what? This sense of ownership boosts their engagement and leads to a deeper understanding and retention of the content. Who said learning couldn't be an epic adventure?

Gamified learning is like the ultimate wingman for collaboration and social interaction. Through multiplayer games, team challenges, and friendly leaderboards, students are not just learning solo, they're part of a learning squad. It's all about teamwork, sharing knowledge, and supporting each other's growth. This collaborative spirit not only boosts their interpersonal skills but also creates a classroom vibe that's positive and inclusive. High fives all around!

And here's the cherry on top: immediate feedback, served fresh from the gamified learning kitchen. Games have this magical ability to offer real-time feedback, giving students a chance to assess their progress on the spot. It's like having a personal cheerleader who's got your back. This timely feedback is crucial for students to understand where they shine and where they can level up their skills. Talk about personalized learning at its finest.

Oh, and let's not forget about motivation. Gamified learning knows how to tap into that intrinsic motivation that's hiding in all of us. With a sprinkle of healthy competition, rewards, and recognition, students become unstoppable. They're not just chasing grades; they're fueled by a passion to excel and achieve their goals. It's like igniting a fire within them that keeps burning long after the class ends. Lifelong learners, here they come!

Now, assessing the effectiveness of gamified learning requires some clever methods. We've got the quantitative approach with pre- and post-tests, measuring academic progress and knowledge retention. But let's not stop there. We can also dive into the qualitative side, gathering insights from student surveys, interviews, and classroom observations. It's like getting the full story, capturing student engagement, collaboration, and motivation in action.

Gamified learning is a game-changer in education. By assessing its effectiveness, we unlock its full potential and create dynamic and inclusive learning environments. The autonomy, collaboration, immediate feedback, and intrinsic motivation it brings empower students to become active participants in their own education. The result? Improved academic outcomes and a genuine passion for learning that will carry them through a lifetime of adventure. Game on!

CHAPTER SEVEN

Overcoming Challenges and Obstacles

Cracking the Resistance Code: Winning Over Students and Colleagues

Let's face it, incorporating gamified learning strategies can sometimes feel like navigating through a field of resistance. Students and colleagues may be hesitant, skeptical, or just plain resistant to the idea. But fear not, because in this section, we've got some expert advice and techniques to help you address and overcome this reluctance like a pro.

When it comes to students, their resistance can stem from various reasons like fear of change, lack of interest, or doubts about gamified learning's effectiveness. So, how do we break through their walls of resistance? The key is clear and engaging communication. Take the time to explain the advantages of gamified learning in a way that sparks their interest. Show them how it can make learning more enjoyable, boost their motivation and engagement, and ultimately improve their academic performance. Share success stories and real-life examples where gamification has made a positive impact on students' learning outcomes. Paint a vivid picture of how gamified learning can turn their educational journey into an epic adventure.

But that's not all. To truly win them over, get them involved in the decision-making process. Seek their input and feedback through surveys or group discussions. Let them know that their opinions matter and give them a sense of ownership over their own learning experience. When students feel like they have a say in how things are done, resistance tends to melt away like ice cream on a sunny day.

Now, let's tackle the resistance from our esteemed colleagues. It can be trickier since they may lack knowledge or understanding about gamified learning. But fear not, brave educator, because you've got the power to change their minds. Start by sparking conversations about the benefits of gamification and share success stories from other educators who have already embraced gamified learning strategies. Be the shining beacon of knowledge and offer to provide training or workshops to demonstrate effective ways of incorporating gamification into the curriculum. Show them the light, and they'll follow.

Collaboration is key when it comes to addressing resistance from colleagues. Invite them to observe your gamified lessons or share resources and materials that they can use to integrate gamified learning into their own classrooms. Encourage open dialogue and create a supportive environment where teachers can freely express their concerns and challenges. Together, you can conquer any obstacle and find collective solutions to make gamified learning a reality.

And let's not forget the power of ongoing support and resources. Offer professional development opportunities like webinars or workshops, where teachers can learn from experts in the field and exchange best practices. Build a treasure trove of gamification resources, including lesson plans, assessment tools, and game-based platforms, to assist teachers in implementing gamified learning with ease. With the right support and resources, resistance doesn't stand a chance.

Addressing resistance from students and colleagues is no easy task, but armed with effective communication, student involvement, training, collaboration, ongoing support, and a sprinkle of perseverance, you can turn the tides. So, go forth, brave educator, and conquer that resistance. Unlock the power of gamified learning and create an engaging and effective learning environment that will leave resistance in the dust. Adventure awaits!

Mastering the Art of Time and Resource Juggling in Gamified Learning

Ah, gamified learning, the perfect blend of education and fun. But let's not forget that successful implementation requires some serious time and resource management skills. Fear not, intrepid educators, because in this section, we'll dive into the world of time and resource management for gamified learning.

When it comes to time management, it's all about finding the sweet spot. You want to strike a balance between traditional instruction and the exciting world of game-based activities. It's like trying to bake the perfect cake – too much traditional instruction and the gamified fun gets neglected, too much gamification and the curriculum goals crumble. So, let's whip up a well-planned schedule that allows for both educational content and thrilling gamified experiences. By thoughtfully allocating time, you can create an educational feast that satisfies both your curriculum goals and your students' hunger for gamified learning.

Effective resource management is the secret ingredient to success. Consider the availability and accessibility of technological tools and games that align with your learning objectives. You want to make sure they play nicely with your curriculum and meet the specific needs of your students. Take the time to explore different platforms and tools that offer gamified learning experiences. Evaluate their effectiveness and suitability for your classroom. It's like choosing the perfect spice blend – you want the flavors to complement each other and create a delicious learning experience.

Now, let's sprinkle some collaboration and professional development into the mix. Connect with fellow educators who have mastered the art of gamified learning. Join professional learning communities where you can share experiences, strategies, and resources. Together, you can unlock the secrets of efficient time and resource management. It's like joining forces with a team of master chefs – you learn from their expertise, swap recipes, and create culinary wonders together.

And don't forget to let your students have a taste of responsibility. Involve them in the decision-making process. Give them a voice in selecting games and deciding how to allocate time for gamified activities. When students take an active role in managing time and resources, they develop a sense of ownership over their learning. It's like giving them a seat at the chef's table – they feel valued and empowered.

So, there you have it, the recipe for effective time and resource management in gamified learning. Carefully plan your time, balance your resources, collaborate with other educators, and empower your students. With these skills, you'll create an engaging and effective learning experience that leaves everyone wanting seconds. Bon appétit!

Navigating the Gamified Learning Maze: Troubleshooting Common Issues

Ah, gamified learning, the land of endless possibilities and engaged students. But wait, even in this fantastical realm, there may be challenges lurking around every corner. Fear not, brave teachers, for in this section, we shall venture forth and conquer the common hurdles that may arise during gamification implementation.

Our first challenge is student disengagement. While gamified learning has the potential to boost motivation, some students may not jump on the gamification bandwagon right away. They may be puzzled by the game mechanics, uninterested in the themes, or simply overwhelmed by the competitive nature of it all. To tackle this, let's sprinkle some personalization into the mix. Allow students to choose avatars or game themes that resonate with their interests. Provide clear instructions and tutorials right from the start, ensuring everyone understands the rules of the game. After all, nobody likes feeling lost in a labyrinth of confusion.

Next up, we face the hurdle of limited resources or technical difficulties. Ah, the technological realm, where dragons of compatibility and glitches await. But fear not, for we have backup plans! If technology is scarce or mischievous, explore alternative options like board games or low-tech game elements that still ignite the spark of gamified learning. Seek the wisdom of the IT department or discover alternative platforms that can slay those technical dragons.

Now, let's navigate the treacherous path of maintaining student motivation and preventing burnout. Ah, the ebb and flow of enthusiasm that can sometimes dwindle over time. But fret not, for we hold the key to renewal! Introduce new challenges, levels, or rewards periodically to keep the game fresh and exciting. Unleash the power of collaboration, where students band together to conquer shared goals. Teamwork makes the dream work, they say.

Last but not least, we face the formidable challenge of assessment and grading. Oh, how traditional grading methods may clash with the gamified realm. But fear not, for we shall forge a new path! Establish clear criteria for earning points or leveling up, guiding students on their quest for success. Provide timely feedback to steer them in the right direction. And hey, let's consider alternative assessment methods, like portfolios or project-based assessments, which can better capture the essence of learning in this gamified adventure.

So, fellow adventurers, as we journey through the realm of gamified learning, let us not fear the challenges that lie ahead. With personalization, resourcefulness, motivation boosts, and innovative assessment, we can conquer any obstacle and create a vibrant and effective gamified learning experience for our students. Onward, to victory!

CHAPTER EIGHT

Success is Within Your Reach

Unleashing the Power of Gamified Learning: Real-Life Classroom Adventures

Picture this: a classroom transformed into an exciting realm where learning becomes an epic quest filled with adventure and discovery. Gamified learning has taken the education world by storm, captivating and motivating students like never before. By infusing game elements into the learning process, teachers are creating immersive environments that foster collaboration, critical thinking, and problem-solving skills. In this section, we embark on a journey through practical examples of gamified learning in action, showcasing its remarkable impact on student learning outcomes.

Let's dive into one captivating example: online platforms that offer gamified learning experiences. Imagine a biology class where students step into a virtual laboratory, conducting experiments and exploring scientific concepts in a safe and engaging environment. By earning points, badges, or leveling up, students are enticed to actively participate, diving deeper into the wonders of biology.

Now, prepare for another adventure! Instead of traditional quizzes or exams, teachers are embracing interactive assessments that bring the excitement of games into the classroom. Imagine a history class transformed into a high-stakes game of Jeopardy, where students compete in teams, answering questions about historical events, figures, and concepts. Learning becomes a thrilling competition, fostering teamwork and igniting the fire of healthy rivalry among students.

Gamified learning has even found its way into classroom management and student behavior. Teachers are wielding the power of point-based reward systems or virtual currencies to incentivize positive behavior and create a sense of accomplishment. In a math class, students earn points for active participation, completing assignments on time, and lending a helping hand to peers. These hard-earned points can then be exchanged for small rewards or privileges, transforming the classroom into a motivating haven of positivity.

These real-life examples demonstrate the immense value of gamified learning. By weaving game elements into the fabric of education, teachers are crafting experiences that ignite student motivation, foster collaboration, and sharpen critical thinking skills. Whether it's through online platforms, game-like assessments, or behavior management systems, gamified learning is transforming the educational landscape. So, let's embrace the power of gamification and embark on this exciting adventure together, unlocking a world of engagement and achievement for our students.

Unlocking the Magic of Gamified Learning: Insights from Teachers and Students

To truly understand the wonders of gamified learning, let's step into the shoes of those who have experienced it firsthand. In this section, we'll dive deep into the heartfelt testimonials of teachers and the enlightening feedback from students, revealing the transformative power of gamification in the classroom.

Teachers who have embraced gamified learning can't help but marvel at the remarkable changes they've witnessed in their students. What was once a sea of disinterest and apathy has been transformed into a lively and engaged group of learners. These teachers have witnessed a surge in student interaction, collaboration, and critical thinking—essential skills for thriving in the modern world.

Take, for example, Mrs. Davis, a high school English teacher and a good friend of mine. She eagerly shares her gamification journey:

> *"Since I introduced gamified learning in my classroom, it's like stepping into a whole new universe. My students have gone from passive observers to active participants in their own education. With the allure of points, badges, and leaderboards, they eagerly tackle tasks, solve problems, and collaborate like never before. The energy and excitement in my classroom have skyrocketed, and their understanding and retention of the content have improved significantly."*

But it's not just the teachers who are singing the praises of gamified learning. Students themselves have voiced their thoughts on the matter, revealing a newfound motivation, empowerment, and investment in their learning journeys. They appreciate the instant feedback provided by gamified platforms, allowing them to track their progress and adjust their strategies accordingly. The element of competition has also added a sprinkle of fun and excitement to their educational adventures.

Let's hear from Maria, a tenth-grade student. She recently shared her experience in a gamified classroom setting:

> *"I used to dread dragging myself to school in the morning, but now I actually look forward to it. Some days, it feels like I'm stepping into a game or a competition rather than a classroom. We earn points, badges, and compete against*

other classes—it's a lot more fun than writing notes or doing worksheets. I'm actually learning new things because I'm having fun. I never would have thought English class could be this enjoyable. I still have some classes I'm not crazy about, but the gamified learning has made getting up in the mornings to go to school a whole lot more bearable."

These heartfelt testimonials and insightful student feedback stand as undeniable proof of the positive impact of gamified learning. By infusing game-like elements into the learning process, teachers create an environment that captures students' hearts and minds, fostering active participation, collaboration, and critical thinking. The transformative nature of gamification not only amplifies students' academic achievements but also nurtures a lifelong love for learning.

Unveiling the Secrets of Successful Gamification: Lessons from the Trenches

In a world where technology evolves faster than you can say "digital revolution," educators face the thrilling challenge of captivating students' attention. Enter gamification—a magical approach that infuses the learning experience with game-like elements, igniting a spark of motivation and propelling students to excel. In this section, let's dive into the insights from successful gamified learning experiences and uncover strategies for implementing them in classrooms to supercharge students' learning outcomes.

Lesson 1: Clear Goals and Objectives:
One of the essential lessons we've learned from successful gamification adventures is the power of setting clear goals and objectives. By giving students a roadmap, a purpose to their learning,

we awaken their inner sense of purpose. Gamified learning thrives when it has a defined mission, be it reinforcing content knowledge or nurturing critical thinking skills. When students know where they're headed, they buckle up and stay engaged throughout the learning journey.

Lesson 2: Meaningful Rewards and Feedback:

Another gem we've unearthed is the significance of meaningful rewards and feedback. Gamification thrives on celebrating progress and achievements. But here's the secret sauce—it's crucial to make those rewards meaningful and in sync with the learning objectives. Whether it's badges, leaderboards, virtual currency, or unlocking new levels or content, rewards should light a fire in students' hearts. And let's not forget timely and constructive feedback—students crave that golden nugget of information to track their progress and level up their skills.

Lesson 3: Collaboration and Competition:

Collaboration and competition take center stage in the tales of victorious gamification. By blending teamwork and friendly rivalry, educators unleash a whirlwind of camaraderie and engagement among students. Picture group challenges that make minds meld, cooperative missions that turn classmates into allies, or competitive quizzes that spark a fire in students' eyes. These strategies fuel collaboration, support, and the pursuit of excellence.

Lesson 4: Flexibility and Adaptability:

Flexibility and adaptability are the secret ingredients to success in the realm of gamification. Educators must embrace the art of refinement and adjustment based on student feedback and outcomes. Creating a safe space where students can share their thoughts and suggestions is key. By remaining open-minded and agile, teachers embark on a never-ending quest to improve their gamified learning experiences and meet the ever-evolving needs of their students.

The treasure trove of successful gamification experiences in education reveals invaluable insights that can catapult student engagement and learning outcomes to new heights. With clear goals, meaningful rewards and feedback, collaboration and competition, and a touch of flexibility and adaptability, teachers unlock an extraordinary learning environment that captures students' hearts and minds. Gamified learning is the enchanted key that empowers educators to inspire their students, nurturing a lifelong love for learning and paving the way for remarkable academic achievements.

CHAPTER NINE

Future Trends and Innovations in Gamified Learning

Unleashing the Power of Emerging Technologies: Gamification on the Rise!

In today's fast-paced digital realm, technology has seamlessly woven itself into the fabric of our daily lives. And the realm of education is no exception. While some schools and districts are still dipping their toes into the pool of modern devices and systems, the potential for growth and innovation is boundless. So, let's embark on an exciting journey and explore the untapped potential of emerging technologies and the thrilling gamification opportunities they bring to the table.

Two stars on the technological horizon that hold immense promise for transforming the classroom experience are virtual reality (VR) and augmented reality (AR). These ingenious inventions whisk students away to virtual realms or overlay digital wonders onto the real world, creating interactive and captivating learning experiences. Picture students donning VR headsets to explore ancient historical sites or manipulating AR overlays to conduct mind-boggling science experiments. The possibilities are as vast as the cosmos itself. By harnessing VR and AR, teachers can infuse lessons with a dose of gamification, sparking curiosity, engagement, and unleashing the full potential of critical thinking and creativity.

Now, let's venture into the realm of artificial intelligence (AI), a technological marvel that promises personalized educational experiences. AI-powered platforms are here to dazzle and adapt to the unique needs of each student, offering tailored learning adventures. Teachers, brace yourselves, for you can wield the power of AI to craft gamified learning pathways that unleash customized challenges and rewards, all tailored to students' performance and progress. The result? Boundless motivation and the power to conquer learning gaps with precision and finesse.

Mobile technology has taken center stage, unveiling a treasure trove of possibilities for gamified learning. Mobile apps and games transform the learning experience, empowering students with anytime, anywhere access to educational delights. Teachers, the stage is set for you to incorporate mobile gamified learning platforms, allowing students to embark on their learning odyssey at their own pace. Collaboration and healthy competition await as students embark on thrilling quests, united in their quest for knowledge. And let's not forget the wonders of game-based assessments, where students can showcase their brilliance through interactive quizzes and simulations. The power is in their hands, quite literally!

As torchbearers of knowledge, it is our sacred duty to embrace these emerging technologies and harness the gamification opportunities they bring forth. Let us weave virtual reality, augmented reality, artificial intelligence, and mobile technology into the tapestry of learning, creating immersive, personalized, and awe-inspiring experiences for our students. Gamified learning becomes the catalyst that fuels their motivation and ignites their thirst for knowledge. And as they delve into the realms of gamification, they emerge equipped with the critical 21st-century skills they need to conquer the challenges of the digital age. Fellow educators, the time has come to unleash the power of emerging technologies and embark on a journey where learning and play intertwine. Let the games begin, and let the adventure unfold!

Embarking on an Adventure with Virtual Reality and Augmented Reality in Education

Note: Before we embark on this exciting journey into the realm of Virtual Reality (VR) and Augmented Reality (AR) in education, it's important to acknowledge that budget constraints can often make acquiring VR and AR gadgets a challenging endeavor for many schools. However, the purpose of this exploration is to inspire and spark ideas that can be adapted to different circumstances. While VR and AR gadgets may not be feasible for everyone, the concepts and principles behind them can still inspire creative solutions that fit within your school's budget. So, let's dive in and discover how we can infuse elements of VR and AR into our classrooms, even if we have to find our own imaginative alternatives. Together, we can unleash the power of gamified learning and create extraordinary educational experiences!

Step right up, ladies and gentlemen, and prepare to have your minds blown by the awe-inspiring wonders of Virtual Reality (VR) and Augmented Reality (AR)! These groundbreaking technologies have taken the world by storm, and education is no exception. Buckle up as we dive into the exciting realm of VR and AR in education, unlocking the doors to immersive and engaging learning experiences like never before.

VR and AR have the power to transport students beyond the confines of the traditional classroom, whisking them away to magical realms where history comes alive, scientific concepts materialize, and imaginary worlds become their playground. With VR, students can witness the wonders of ancient civilizations, explore distant planets, or even shrink down to the size of a molecule. Meanwhile, AR enriches the real world by superimposing digital marvels onto everyday objects, turning textbooks into interactive gateways to knowledge.

The magic of VR and AR lies in their ability to cater to the diverse learning styles and preferences of our students. Visual learners find solace in the immersive, eye-catching landscapes and lifelike experiences that these technologies offer. Meanwhile, kinesthetic learners can jump right in, actively engaging and manipulating virtual objects. By appealing to multiple senses, VR and AR bring abstract concepts to life and cement them in students' minds.

VR and AR foster collaboration and sharpen problem-solving skills. Picture a virtual world where students join forces to tackle complex challenges, conduct virtual experiments, or unravel mind-bending puzzles. The shared experiences and teamwork in multiplayer VR or collaborative AR environments ignite the spark of critical thinking and camaraderie. And fear not, dear teachers, for you hold the power to provide real-time feedback and guidance as you witness their virtual adventures unfold before your very eyes.

Now, before we strap on our VR headsets and don our AR goggles, let's pause for a moment of reflection. Implementing VR and AR in education requires careful consideration. We must ponder the costs, technical requirements, and ethical implications of their usage. It's vital that we harness these technologies to enhance the learning experience and align them with our curriculum goals, rather than getting lost in the glitz and glamor of novelty.

When VR and AR seamlessly integrate into education, a world of possibilities unfolds before us. These transformative technologies immerse students in captivating experiences, ignite their curiosity, and fuel collaboration. Whether it's a journey to the depths of the ocean or a walk through the annals of history, VR and AR open doors to comprehension, engagement, and exploration like never before.

So, grab your VR headsets, don your AR goggles, and embark on this thrilling adventure into the realm of gamified learning with VR and AR as your trusty companions. Together, let's create an educational environment that inspires, excites, and empowers our students to reach for the stars and achieve their fullest potential.

The Potential of Gamified Learning for Personalized Education

Gamified learning: the superhero of personalized education! It swoops in, capes flapping, to transform the traditional classroom into an interactive and individualized learning extravaganza. By infusing game elements into the educational experience, teachers become the architects of an engaging and immersive world where students are the heroes of their own learning journeys.

One of the fantastic powers of gamified learning is its ability to adapt and cater to each student's unique needs. No more one-size-fits-all approach! With gamification, teachers can customize content, challenges, and feedback to match the superpowers and progress of each student. It's like having a personal tutor for every student, guiding them through their academic adventures.

Gamified learning brings teamwork and collaboration to center stage. Just like the Avengers joining forces, educational games often include multiplayer features that encourage students to work together towards a common goal. Through collaboration, students learn from one another, developing their communication, critical thinking, and problem-solving skills. It's like a classroom full of superheroes, using their powers collectively to save the day!

And let's not forget the joy factor. Learning should be an exciting roller coaster ride, not a dull and monotonous slog. That's where gamification shines. By tapping into our natural love for challenges, achievements, and rewards, gamified learning transforms education into an amusement park of knowledge. When students are having fun, they become more than passive learners – they become active participants, fully engaged and eager to conquer new educational heights.

Now, let's not get carried away by the superhero hype. Gamified learning is not a magical cure-all. It requires thoughtful planning and implementation. Teachers need to carefully select and design gamified activities that align with learning objectives and curriculum guidelines. And like any good superhero, they must constantly assess their strategies, making tweaks and adjustments as needed to ensure maximum impact.

Unleash the power of gamified learning and let it soar through your classrooms. Embrace the potential for personalized education, where students take charge of their learning, collaborate like superheroes, and find joy in their academic pursuits. With gamification as your trusty sidekick, the future of education is brighter than ever!

CHAPTER TEN

Reflection and Next Steps

Reflecting on the Impact of Gamified Learning

Gamified learning: the secret ingredient that turns education into an exciting adventure! It's like sprinkling magic dust over the classroom, instantly captivating students and fueling their passion for learning. Let's take a moment to reflect on the incredible impact gamified learning has on our students.

One of the superpowers of gamified learning is its ability to unleash student engagement. By introducing game mechanics like points, badges, and leaderboards, teachers create an environment that is more thrilling than a rollercoaster ride. Students are hooked, eager to participate, and compete for the top spot. And guess what? This heightened engagement leads to deeper learning, critical thinking, and a genuine love for acquiring knowledge.

But that's not all. Gamified learning also comes with its own built-in superhero: immediate feedback! With interactive quizzes, simulations, and challenges, students get instant feedback on their performance. It's like having a personal cheerleader by their side, guiding them on their learning journey. Armed with this feedback, students can reflect on their mistakes, make improvements, and unleash their full potential. Talk about a confidence boost!

Let's not forget about the incredible power of collaboration. Gamified learning platforms bring students together like a well-oiled superhero team. They can join forces, tackle challenges, and conquer the world of knowledge together. Through collaboration, students develop essential skills like communication, teamwork, and empathy, preparing them to be real-world superheroes.

And here's the cherry on top: autonomy and choice. Gamified learning puts students in the driver's seat of their education. They get to choose their own learning path, make decisions, and take ownership of their learning experience. It's like giving them a personalized superhero cape that empowers them to explore, create, and conquer any academic challenge that comes their way.

By harnessing the power of gamified learning, we transform the classroom into an epic battleground of knowledge. With heightened engagement, immediate feedback, collaboration, and a sense of autonomy, we create an educational environment where students can unleash their inner superheroes. So, teachers, let's embrace the magic of gamified learning and embark on an extraordinary journey of student growth and success. Together, we can change the world—one game at a time!

Strategies for Continual Improvement in Gamification

So you've gamified your classroom and the students are loving it. But here's the thing: to keep the momentum going and ensure long-term success, you've got to level up your gamification game. Let's dive into some strategies for continual improvement that will keep the excitement alive!

First up, regular evaluation and feedback. Take a step back and assess how your gamification strategies are working. Are they hitting the mark or falling flat? Seek feedback from your students and colleagues to get a fresh perspective. Their insights can be pure gold and help you fine-tune your approach.

Next, be adaptable and flexible. Just like a skilled gamer adjusts their strategy on the fly, be ready to tweak your gamification techniques.

Stay open to incorporating new game mechanics, challenges, or rewards that better align with your learning objectives and student interests. It's all about keeping things fresh and exciting.

Collaboration is key, my friend. Integrate multiplayer game elements that encourage teamwork, communication, and problem-solving. Throw in some group challenges, cooperative quests, or friendly competitions. Not only will it build camaraderie among your students, but it'll also give them the chance to level up their collaboration skills.

Remember, personalization is the name of the game. Customize the gamified learning experience to meet the needs of each student. Let them progress at their own pace, earn rewards based on their achievements, and choose activities that align with their interests. When students have ownership over their learning, they'll be motivated to keep playing and conquering those educational challenges.

And don't forget about your own professional development. Gamification is a dynamic field, always evolving. Stay in the loop by attending workshops, conferences, or online courses that focus on gamified learning. Sharpen those skills and stay ahead of the game.

By implementing these strategies for continual improvement, you'll keep your gamification mojo going strong. Your classroom will be buzzing with engagement, collaboration, and personalization. So get out there, embrace the power of gamification, and let the learning adventure continue!

Inspiring Teachers to Embrace Gamified Learning

We all know how challenging it can be to capture our students' attention and keep them engaged, but fear not! The power of play and games is here to save the day.

Gamified learning is all about infusing elements of games into our teaching methods to create an immersive and enjoyable learning experience. By tapping into students' natural love for games, we can ignite their curiosity and passion for learning like never before.

One of the remarkable benefits of gamified learning is its ability to foster active participation and collaboration among students. With features like leaderboards, badges, and levels, we can create a fun and healthy dose of competition and teamwork. Not only will this enhance their problem-solving and critical-thinking skills, but it will also empower them to take ownership of their learning journey.

But that's not all! Gamified learning offers immediate feedback, allowing students to track their progress and identify areas where they can level up. By rewarding their accomplishments along the way, we inspire them to keep pushing forward and reaching for the stars.

Now, let's talk about practicality. Implementing gamified learning requires thoughtful planning and design. We'll explore strategies and examples that align with your curriculum and learning objectives. Don't worry, we'll cover digital tools and platforms for all comfort levels, so no one gets left behind.

By embracing gamified learning, we'll create a classroom culture that values creativity, collaboration, and critical thinking. We'll transform our teaching practices and inspire our students to become active, motivated, and lifelong learners. It's an adventure worth taking!

Conclusion

As we come to the end of "Game On: Level Up Your Teaching," I hope this journey into the world of gamified learning has sparked your imagination and filled you with excitement. Throughout this book, we have explored the potential of gamification to transform the educational landscape and enhance the learning experience for our students.

We began by delving into the fundamentals of gamification, understanding its core principles and the psychology behind its effectiveness. We discovered that by incorporating game elements into our teaching, we can unlock a world of engagement, motivation, and collaboration within our classrooms.

From designing gamified lessons to implementing effective strategies, we have learned how to create dynamic and immersive learning experiences. We have explored the importance of aligning gamification with curriculum objectives, providing meaningful challenges, and fostering a positive classroom culture that encourages growth and exploration.

We have also explored a wide range of digital tools, platforms, and resources that support gamified learning, understanding that technology can amplify our efforts and offer endless possibilities for creative and interactive experiences. Remember, these tools are not just for students but can also be a source of inspiration and support for us as educators.

Throughout our journey, we have uncovered the numerous benefits of gamified learning. We have witnessed the power of increased student engagement, motivation, collaboration, critical thinking, and academic achievement. We have seen how gamification can tap into students' natural curiosity, transforming the learning process into an adventure filled with joy, discovery, and growth.

Now, as we reach the end, I urge you to take what you have learned and put it into action. Embrace gamified learning as a powerful tool in your teaching arsenal. Take those first steps towards gamifying your lessons, creating immersive experiences, and empowering your students to become active participants in their own education.

Remember, the journey will have its challenges. You may encounter obstacles or face moments of doubt. But with each challenge, there is an opportunity for growth. As educators, we have the power to adapt, iterate, and refine our gamification strategies. We can learn from our students, experiment with new ideas, and continually evolve as we discover what works best for our unique classrooms.

So, my fellow educators, I encourage you to embark on your own gamification journey. Embrace the joy of teaching and learning, infuse your lessons with game-like elements, and watch as your students' enthusiasm soars. Let your creativity run wild, and don't be afraid to take risks. Remember, the greatest rewards often come from stepping outside our comfort zones.

Together, let us transform education and create vibrant, engaging, and meaningful learning experiences. Let us embrace gamified learning as a catalyst for student growth, inspiration, and lifelong love for learning. The power is in your hands. Level up your teaching and let the games begin!

Resources:

Getting Started with Gamification

The following are a handful of resources that are great for gamifying learning! I am, by no means, endorsing any particular service, although I've used quite a few of these myself. I am providing this list as a means of helping you get started on your own gamification journey.So, roll up your sleeves and embark on your own exploration to discover resources that will bring fun and engagement into your classroom!

BreakoutEDU.com: If you're looking for educational games and puzzles that will bring excitement to your classroom, BreakoutEDU.com is the place to go. With a wide range of subjects and grade levels covered, this website offers engaging and interactive learning experiences that will leave your students eager for more.

Brainpop.com: Dive into the world of Brainpop.com, where educational games, videos, and quizzes await. Explore various subjects and topics while having fun and expanding your knowledge.

Classcraft.com: Transform your classroom into an epic adventure with Classcraft. This web-based platform empowers students to create their own characters, form teams, and earn points for academic and social skills. Meanwhile, teachers have the tools they need to manage classroom behavior, track student progress, and communicate with parents. It's a win-win for everyone involved!

Classdojo.com: Say hello to Class Dojo, your digital classroom companion. This website allows you to create personalized and engaging classrooms where students can earn points for positive behaviors and skills. With features like feedback sharing, photo and video sharing, and direct messaging with parents, Class Dojo makes it easy to motivate students and foster a collaborative and improved learning environment.

Dreamscape.com: Unleash your imagination with Dreamscape.com. This website lets teachers create captivating games tailored to their students' needs. The games are designed to align with curriculum standards and offer an interactive and enjoyable way for students to learn and practice various skills.

Duolingo.com: Get ready to embark on a language-learning adventure with Duolingo. This app turns language learning into a game, where you earn points, level up, and unlock new skills. With bite-sized lessons and a focus on speaking, listening, reading, and writing, Duolingo makes language learning fun and addictive.

Edulastic.com: Looking for interactive and engaging assessments? Look no further than Edulastic.com. This platform empowers teachers to create assessments that captivate students and make learning come alive.

Kahoot.com: Prepare for some interactive and fast-paced fun with Kahoot!. This website lets you create and play quizzes, polls, and surveys in real time. Whether you're in the classroom or remote, Kahoot! enhances learning and engagement. Join live games hosted by others or challenge yourself with solo play.

Quizizz.com: Say goodbye to boring quizzes and hello to Quizizz.com. This website adds a playful twist to learning by allowing educators to create and play interactive quizzes with their students. It's a great tool for gamifying the learning experience, motivating students to participate, compete, and have a blast while learning.

Quizlet.com: Flashcards and memorization just got a whole lot more enjoyable with Quizlet. This website offers a variety of interactive games, flashcards, and tests to help you study different subjects. Join study groups, compete with other learners, and take your learning to the next level.

Socrative.com: Looking to spice up your classroom with interactive quizzes, polls, and games? Socrative.com has got you covered. Engage your students in friendly competition, provide instant feedback, and reward their progress with this web-based platform designed to gamify learning.

There's a whole world of resources out there that I haven't even touched upon. The beauty of gamifying your classroom is that you get to shape your own vision and discover the tools that perfectly fit your teaching style and your students' needs. It's time to dive in and start exploring. Experiment, tinker, and find what works best for you. And when you find that resource that aligns with your goals and makes your gamified learning experience even better, you'll know you've hit the jackpot.

So go ahead, have a blast, and let the gamification adventure begin!

Education
Unboxed
EMPOWER YOUR TEACHING

Unpack. Discover. Explore.

Check out Education Unboxed for teaching

and learning resources, articles, and more!

www.educationunboxed.co

Printed in Great Britain
by Amazon

46036526R00050

PORKY'S BRIDGE

D.J. Forbes

MINERVA PRESS
ATLANTA LONDON SYDNEY

ISBN 0 75410 763 9

First Published 1999 by
MINERVA PRESS
315–317 Regent Street
London W1R 7YB

Printed in Great Britain for Minerva Press

PORKY'S BRIDGE

Chapter One

My wife had arranged for me to pick up our granddaughter who would be staying with us for a couple of weeks during her summer holidays. The drive back home was long and the M25 quickly became a car park because of cones on parade. I decided to make a detour, in the faint hope that if the car kept moving, my passenger wouldn't be bored out of her mind. As I drove through the most northern parts of Greater London, Jessica assumed I had lost direction, and was driving round in a muddle.

'No I'm not lost Jessica,' I chuckled, 'I was born round this way.'

'Oh,' remarked Jessica. She leant forward and lowered the volume on the radio.

'Wasn't Nan born round this way too, Granddad?'

'That's right,' I replied.

The car came to a halt at the roundabout by the River Lea in Ponders End.

'So how did you and Nan get it together then? Was it love at first sight?' Jessica probed.

'Hardly,' I said, and pulled away swiftly.

'This music is boring,' said Jessica, and she switched the radio off. 'Go on Granddad – how did you meet Nan?' Jessica asked, as she nestled back into her seat.

We had the best part of our journey before us and if Jessica was interested I thought, why not tell the tale to whittle the time away and make the long journey more tolerable. I suppose you could say that it was the two weeks before the school summer holidays in 1957 that were the shaping of our fate together really. You could say that period, when Rock 'n' Roll made its impact on us kids, laid the groundwork towards us being an item, to use the modern term. Our lifestyle and attitudes were completely different back then, especially living on a huge estate. Imagine four boys whose sole aim was to play practical jokes on all and sundry; real pranksters that were forever laughing and enjoying themselves, though they never went out of their way to hurt anybody with the pranks they pulled.

Friday nights were always spent at the local cinema, the Premier. We kids called it the Bughutch because of its undesirable reputation, fleas supposedly jumped from head to head and bug-like insects scampered under the rows of seats. If you went to watch a B film, by the end of the A film you would be itching all over your body.

Most of it was hearsay and us kids added to that with exaggerated tales of eerie ghosts appearing in the darkness... back in those days it was all part of the excitement for us kids on a Friday night.

You'd be surprised how many kids were frightened of those tales.

Most times, when the cinema chucked out, we kids would all go to the fish and chip shop for a bag of chips to eat on the way home.

One Friday night in particular, there was a new glass oven in the chip shop window roasting chickens on a revolving spit, it was all the fashion back then.

Barley and Danny enquired on the price of a quarter of chicken but soon realised that they couldn't afford such luxuries. Being a resourceful pair of characters that weren't going to be thwarted by mere details, they came up with the bright idea of roasting their own chickens. As it so happened, Bob, their mutual neighbour, kept chickens in his garden to supply himself with freshly laid eggs. Barley and Danny set about devising a plan to bag two birds from Bob.

Early on Monday morning before leaving for school, Barley stood by the kitchen window watching Bob potter about by the chicken shed.

Bob's no pushover, thought Barley, he was shrewd, shrewd enough to have a bunch of kids of various ages, from the estate, pose with him for a photograph as his own children. This was so when passengers bought tickets for their train journeys, and waved for a porter, Bob having hauled their luggage into the carriage, would then show them the photograph, and feed them a sob story: The passengers would then feel compelled to cough up a shiny cure.

Barley also noticed Mrs Mantle lugging her washing up the garden path. Unable to resist needling his next door neighbour, Barley snatched his jacket off the kitchen table, thread one arm through the sleeve and opened the back door.

'Don't slam the back door,' warned Barley's mother.

'Course I won't,' he replied, shutting the door with a bang! 'Morning Bob,' said Barley, adjusting the collar on his jacket.

'Morning, young Barley,' mumbled Bob, and sauntered up the garden path towards his young neighbour. He came to a halt by the garden fence, hooked a thumb in his waistcoat pocket, looked down and then up at the chicken shed and prodded his finger. 'I don't understand it. The chickens haven't laid any eggs for two days,' he said, in disgust, anchoring another thumb into the pocket so that both arms then hung limp. He then gazed at Barley, 'Why do you think that is?' he asked.

'I don't know,' Barley replied, leaning against the fence and turning to look across at Mrs Mantle. 'Good morning my fine washer lady or peg lady,' he said, with a teasing sparkle in his eye.

Mrs Mantle wasn't a happy-go-lucky character at the best of times and she peered back over the top of her glasses in contempt. Having none of his banter, she replied in one breath, 'Barley... all right Bob,' and carried on pegging her washing onto the line.

Bob gave a short wave of acknowledgement, but was still puzzled. 'That's two days that I haven't had any eggs – that's unusual that is,' Bob declared, shaking his head in disbelief. 'I enjoy eggs for me breakfast I do,' he added.

Barley's mischievous interest hovered over Mrs Mantle, as her son's radiant, white shirts floated in the breeze. 'Let's hope the birds don't dive-bomb Bobby's white shirts, Mrs Mantle,' said Barley, 'Bobby wouldn't like that would he? Mind you, he could always say to his boss, "I have my white shirts monogrammed you know."' Pleased that he'd started the day off on the right note, Barley turned to Bob, and didn't catch Mrs Mantle's thrusting two-fingered response from behind her washing. 'I've just had a thought, now you mention it, Bob. Perhaps your chickens are saving eggs for one big hatch, you know like those African chickens; it's supposed to be lucky you know.'

Bob noted Barley's sincere expression and pretended to give the subject some consideration.

'I don't think so,' he said and shook his head. 'No, no, no, I'm sure these chickens wouldn't do that.'

'Oh, they would, Bob,' assured Barley. 'We're having lessons on this subject at school – this very day in fact. I'm becoming an expert on chickens,' adding convincingly, 'I know what I'm talking about, Bob.'

There must *be* African chickens, but what have they in common with the chickens in my shed? thought Bob and gave the matter more contemplation, despite changing the subject entirely. 'Was it true that there was a big commotion down the Izaac Walton on Saturday night?' asked Bob.

Considering that news spread through the estate faster than running water, and that old Bob was as canny as canny could be, he'd probably heard all the gossip already, mused Barley.

'Not many there was,' replied Barley. 'A right big bundle. I'd gone down to fetch some seafood from the stall when I heard the punch-up start in the pub. Then, it came brawling out of the door. By that time I was sat on the wall eating mussels. Old man Butcher can't half fight though – he gave three of them a good hiding before the police arrived and threw him into the meat wagon. Mind you, it took four coppers to do so.'

'It's beyond a joke,' said Bob. 'It's becoming traditional; every Saturday night the same behaviour. That's why I gave up having me pint there and buying me crab from the stall.'

'Well! It's time I had a word with mother Mantle over there,' said Barley, hoping to prompt Bob back to his chicken theory.

Bob gazed down at a couple of pebbles by his feet and flicked them off the path. 'All right then,' he replied.

Barley, thinking his bait had failed, stepped back from the fence.

'By the way,' said Bob, beckoning his young neighbour closer, 'what was you saying about your lessons at school? Something to do with chickens wasn't it?'

Barley wanted to jump for joy, knowing full well Bob knew nothing about chickens, except they laid eggs which he ate. As that was all he seemed concerned about, Barley could spin Bob a yarn as long as a crooked mile.

'That's right. The evolution of chickens – a sort of potted history really. Before they became domesticated, chickens could fly, you know? Chickens today are not much different. Back in those days, tribe people thought that chickens were very intelligent animals but you'd know all about that, wouldn't you Bob?'

'So you think the fact that my chickens have laid no eggs, goes back all those years?' asked Bob, with a crafty glance.

'Very likely, very likely indeed… and very lucky for you I might tell you.'

'Why's that?' Bob enquired curtly, peering over his nose at Barley.

'I don't have all the answers as yet – not until we have the rest of our lessons today.'

'Barley!' said Bob, lowering his voice. As he hunched his shoulders, his eyes gleamed from behind narrow lids, and his fat cheeks bulged with a smile. 'Lucky you say?'

Barley glanced both ways, then leaned over the fence, and whispered, 'Very lucky: a good omen for you all right. I tell you what, let me find out more from school today, and I'll put you wise tonight.'

Bob seemed pleased with that idea and patted Barley on the shoulder. 'See you tonight,' he whispered, smiled, and trundled back to the house.

'No problem,' Barley muttered under his breath, and headed across the garden to have some more verbal swipes at Mrs Mantle.

Clasping his hands on a round-headed concrete post, he rested his chin on the backs of his hands, and yawned. 'Still minding everybody's business, Mrs Mantle?'

'Not so much of your lip, Barley,' she growled, 'or I'll tell your father.'

Mrs Mantle couldn't see Barley from behind the washing on the line, so he pulled a face and poked his tongue out. 'It's only what me dad says anyway,' he said. 'All the family think so; sister, aunts, uncles, grandparents, even me dad's horse. He's heard you with those long ears of his: the horse that is, not me dad!'

Mrs Mantle remained tight-lipped, and continued pegging the last item of clothing on the line. She then picked up the empty bowl and appeared from behind the washing line, an arm's length from Barley.

'I'm only joking, Mrs Mantle,' said Barley, with both hands up in surrender.

'It's a good job you are,' she frowned, 'or you'd cop it, I can tell you.'

'Oh I *was*, Mrs Mantle,' said Barley and with a wide smile added, 'Horses don't understand your gossip.'

As quick as a flash, Mrs Mantle threw the remaining water in the bowl all over Barley.

'That'll teach you, you cheeky young blighter. You wait till I see your father,' she huffed and with a sideways glare at Barley, headed back up the garden path.

Barley, not wanting to be caught by his mother with wet clobber on, or he would have quite some explaining to do, made a quick exit out the back gate and went to call for Danny.

Mrs Cade wasn't given to opening the front door to just anyone, so Barley rapped on the front door and stood back down off the step. He cast his gaze over to the window as Mrs Cade fingered back the curtains, pushed her face to the window and recognised Barley.

'You *know*,' she grumbled, indicating with her thumb for him to sling his hook round to the back garden. She then let the curtains swing back into position, and left Barley to jump over the garden fence, and make his own way down the alleyway to the back gate.

Danny was at the bottom of his garden, sat on the roof of his father's shed, cutting a leather tongue from an old, worn-out boot. Aware of Barley approaching, he concentrated harder on the old boot.

'All right, Barley,' said Danny. 'I saw you talking to Bob earlier. How did you get on?'

'Not bad,' Barley replied, clambering onto the top of the shed and sat himself down next to Danny.

'Here, hold the end of this tongue will you, whilst I cut it.'

With a decisive slice, the tongue parted company from the rest of the boot, and was ready for the next stage of producing a pouch.

'Bob swallowed the chicken story, hook, line and sinker. All I've got to do is pile it on a bit more tonight.'

'You can't fail,' said Danny. 'He was born in the last century, what does he know? They never went to school in those days.' Danny grinned.

Barley, inspired by Danny's confidence in his ability to fool Bob, lay back on his elbows, looked skyward, and replied, 'He's so gullible you know...' pausing for a moment in self admiration. 'By the way,' he said, 'how many eggs did you collect this morning?'

Danny put his fingers up and replied, 'Three big whoppers, and without a cluck from the hens or the old cockerel.'

'Great! Looks like roast chicken for Sunday dinner then,' said Barley, counting his chickens before they had hatched. 'I can taste it now...'

'Two roast chickens for dinner,' retorted Danny in surprise that only one had been mentioned. He carried on gouging out two holes in each end of the pouch.

'That's a big enough pouch,' said Barley, exercising one leg in the air. 'What you gonna catapult, boulders?'

'See this?' said Danny. 'It's going to be one big catapult, with two strands of rubber on either side.'

'Don't tell me. It's for shooting aeroplanes down with,' said Barley and laughed.

'You can laugh, but it's better than that,' said Danny. He jumped to his feet. 'Can you see where Porky lives from here?'

Barley got to his feet and stood next to Danny.

Peering over sprawled sheds in back gardens and through gaps in the trees, they could just make out the back gardens of the terraced houses overlooking the park.

'See the shed at the bottom of his garden?' asked Danny, pointing.

'Gotcha,' replied Barley, with a nod of his head.

'By the time I've finished with this catapult, I'll be able to stand on this shed and smash every pane of glass over there.'

'I'm all for it,' Barley said, though in some doubt, 'But that's some distance away – you'll need to be Hercules to pull that catapult back.'

'Lean on me,' said Danny. 'We'll muller it.'

'I hope you're right,' said Barley hesitantly, but added, 'Yes why not, we'll knock every pane of glass out faster than his old man can put them in.'

'That's the spirit,' said Danny and punched a triumphant fist in the air.

Mrs Cade, a stickler for punctuality, came into the garden and with a ear shattering shrill, reminded them that it was time for school.

'I bet you Bomber heard that from his house,' chuckled Danny, and added, 'Well I hope he did.' Implying that Bomber was never on time for school.

Bomber loathed his nickname and cringed every time the story was told of how he acquired it on Coronation Day. The children had finished in the fancy dress competition and were eager to play the games that the adults had organised for them. Bomber however, had had other ideas, and when the games got under way, he had sloped off to his back garden shed for his fishing net. The cane rod measured no taller than himself, and wasn't long enough for the use *he* intended, so he improvised. He dragged an old, metal chest lying in the garden, over to the fence and began fishing in his neighbour's fish pond. The pond was so deep that he couldn't reach to net any fish. Again and again he tried, but the fish swam even deeper. Eventually, Bomber had had enough, and his ideas on fishing expanded. With careful consideration he came up with the ideal solution, bringing the bottom of the pond nearer to the top. To this end, he began lobbing house-bricks into the pond, along with anything else that sank like a depth charge.

When Bill (Bomber's Father) caught him in the act, he screamed out, 'Stop bombing the fish!' Bill unable to understand what on earth possessed his son to lob house-bricks at poor, defenceless fish, demanded an explanation. Bomber's reasoning was very simple. 'I was trying to make them insecure Dad,' he said, 'make them swim in me net. It would have worked. Just a few more house-bricks, and I would have had 'em.'

Bomber thought his nickname would have slipped into obscurity after four years, especially now that he was like any other kid on the estate, fashion conscious and trendy.

Barley and Danny stood at the front gate and called again, mainly to irritate Bomber even more. 'Bomber, Bomber, come on, Zip is waiting.'

Bomber swept his hair back, parted his fingers like a two-pronged pitchfork, ruffled the front of his hair over his forehead, and with one last glance at his reflection in the mirror, stepped out of the back door. Pinching his lapels between his forefingers and thumbs, he slipped his jacket slightly off his shoulders and strutted out from the alleyway as bold as brass. 'Well! I got me new drainpipe trousers on,' he said, grinning.

Barley and Danny's jaws dropped in amazement, as Bomber stepped out in full view on the pavement. Wearing a light grey jacket over a black shirt, Bomber's trousers hugged the contours of his legs tightly, making them look spindly and his feet look huge. 'I told you, I'd be the first to wear them,' he declared, and admired himself with a grin of approval. 'Great aren't they?' he added waiting for Barley and Danny's compliments.

Both boys stood gaping in utter disbelief. They then nudged each other, and burst out laughing.

'Go on, you can laugh. "Let's get Bomber time" is it? You're just jealous,' he growled indignantly and walked ahead.

Barley and Danny knew that Bomber had long preached that he would be the first in fashion but they had never seen drainpipe trousers so tight. Bomber, wondering if it really was jealousy or merely jesting on their behalf, turned round to face them and walked back.

'All right then. What's the matter with my drainpipes?' he asked seriously, expecting favourable criticism.

Danny pointed to Bomber's trousers and blurted. 'They're ballet tights.'

Barley fell to his knees in fits of laughter.

'I still reckon you lot are jealous,' said Bomber, and walked ahead in a huff.

Coming to a halt, he looked back defiantly at Barley and Danny, still laughing with tears in their eyes, 'We'll see what Zip has to say, I'll bet he likes them,' announced Bomber.

Zip's house was close to the far end house overlooking the park, so by the time they had reached the front gate, a more sombre mood prevailed. Bomber, however, felt conspicuous: unsure whether his trousers really did look peculiar, he stood behind Barley and Danny. Zip had seen the boys sauntering along from his bedroom window, and before they had chance to call out, the front door opened.

'You're late,' he said, slammed the front door behind him and trundled down the garden path.

'Just a bit,' replied Danny with snigger not daring to mention Bomber's trousers.

Zip didn't notice Bomber's trousers at first, he was pre-occupied with the mice he'd captured in the fields over the weekend. Danny winked, and with a frantic indication of his head, drew Zip's attention to Bomber's drainpipes. 'Unbelievable,' he said. 'I've never seen trousers like that before. Who gave you them? Whoever it was, they've got a good sense of humour, as do you for wearing them.'

Bomber gave a contemptuous grin. Barley and Danny sniggered, pretending not to take any notice.

'Don't tell me who gave you them,' said Zip, 'let me guess. I've got it – it was a hypnotist; you're hypnotised. You wouldn't wear them otherwise, unless of course you think you're a ballet dancer!'

'Enough wise cracks,' snarled Bomber.

Barley, Danny and Zip rolled about laughing, and Bomber's cheeks glowed red with embarrassment.

'You wait you lot,' said Bomber. 'Your turn will come, 'specially you Danny, when you get your Baseball Boots.'

''Least his feet won't look two sizes bigger,' replied Zip.

'Ha, ha,' sneered Bomber, and recalled how he had laughed at giving Zip his nickname.

It was on a day in late November of the previous year. A fog had settled, far thicker than any the boys had ever seen, so dense it was almost yellow. Trains, buses, cars, and lorries had come to a complete halt and the street lights were only visible when standing close by. Even then, visibility was impaired. Every boy and girl on the estate however, thought the weather conditions ideal for playing outings. Word had spread through the grapevine, that there was to be a meeting at seven o'clock that night by the lamp post, on the corner of the avenue and terrace opposite the park. By seven thirty, a mixture of boys and girls were huddled round the lamp post. All were excited and eager to play outings. Amid the hullabaloo, they managed to organise themselves into two separate teams, the Home team and the Away team. Five of the home team remained as guards round the lamp post (the prison), whilst the remaining team members become hunters, searching for the Away team. The boundaries agreed by both teams for that night included the park, the entire estate (back gardens were out of bounds) front gardens and alleyways. All other areas were excluded, including the allotments opposite the school. The Away team had to split in units of no less than two but no more than four. The Home team (hunters) could scout in packs or as they chose and could apply any method or means to catch their quarry. When a hunter detained a prey, it would be patted on the head three times, and then sent to prison. Prisoner's could be freed if a member of their own team ran into prison and tapped the inmates on the head three times. However, no more than two Away team members at any one time could attempt such a rescue mission. Guards however, could use any means at their disposal to prevent prisoners from escaping. Once all the Away team had been captured all roles would then be reversed.

Although the rules were quite straightforward, most of the competitors would add sparkle to the game by using their stealth and prowess to taunt the hunters. They would leap out from the shadows, front gardens, hide-outs, or simply try and outrun the hunter.

That night the hunters selected Margaret as Captain; she was school champion in sprinting, gymnastics and swimming, and was a match for any boy or girl on the estate.

Barley, thinking the heavy fog would scupper any detection from the Home team, ran off into the park shouting, 'Maggot is the Captain, and Thunder Thighs is a lanky grub!' He was joined in the ridicule by Bomber, Danny, and Zip. Out of sight from the hunters, they agreed to add some extra fun into the game, so closing their eyes, they started twirling round until they fell over, completely disorientated.

Meanwhile, Margaret had taken umbrage and was seething at their cutting remarks, so gave priority for them to be captured first. She employed all her team as hunters, (there was no need for guards as nobody had yet been captured) and instructed them to encircle the perimeters of the park, working towards the centre.

Barley, Bomber, Danny and Zip were wandering around, their sense of direction lost completely.

'Eerie,' said Bomber, 'Maggot will never find us.'

Zip's composure was spooked, and he was glancing constantly over his shoulder.

'You can taste sulphur,' said Bomber and licked his lips.

'Sinister,' said Danny, and nudged Bomber.

'Listen,' said Bomber. 'Did you's hear that?'

'Hear what? What did you hear?' blurted Zip, his eyes scanning nervously around.

'I heard,' Bomber paused and flapped his arms… 'Flapping wings.'

'In thick fog?' snarled Zip.

'Shh… whisper,' said Bomber and elbowed Barley. 'The Devil. He'd fly on a night like this,' said Bomber.

'You could be right,' said Danny and glared at Zip.

'Have you ever seen fog like this before, Zip?' asked Barley.

'It's freezing,' said Zip, and shivered, his teeth chattering. He pulled his collar up under his chin.

Bomber unfastened his buttons and opened his jacket. 'You must be joking. I'm starting to sweat.'

'Yeah, it's hot,' agreed Barley.

'It's hot all right,' said Danny. He began undoing his coat.

'It has to be the Devil's doing,' said Bomber. 'You're the only one freezing, Zip, I'm hot, really hot. Something strange is happening.'

Bomber removed his jacket and threw it over his shoulder.

'If anything came at you now, it could snatch what it wanted and be gone; specially if it had big claws.'

Zip thrust both hands deep into his pockets, with no intention of looking up at any of the other boys.

'It could want *you*, Zip,' said Bomber.

Zip didn't reply, and the boys knew he was ripe for a laugh at his expense.

'We'll make a circle with water and protect ourselves,' said Bomber, and winked at Barley and Danny.

'Like in the comics,' said Barley.

'No,' said Danny. 'Like in Dennis Wheatley. My sister reads all his books.'

'They pour holy water in a circle and stand in it,' said Bomber. 'As we haven't got any holy water, we'll have to urinate and say a prayer.'

'I'm busting to go,' said Danny, trying to keep a straight face.

'It will have to do,' said Bomber. 'You go first, Zip, and we'll line up behind you. When you've emptied your bladder, we can take over. Remember to urinate anticlockwise. Oh yes, don't forget to say a prayer.'

With his collar pulled up tight under his chin, Zip fumbled with his trousers and the boys could hear the sound of urine as it hit the ground. Bomber stretched his arms out, and crept backwards with the two boys behind him. They could just see the faint silhouette of Zip, and on the count of 'three', they let out a deafening scream. Zip's legs danced as though they were on fire, and he let out a yell that would have put a foghorn to shame. However in his panic to pull up the zipper on his trousers, he pinched a vital part of his anatomy, and let out a further shrieking yelp.

Conscious of loud fits of laughter coming from behind him, he realised he'd been caught in more ways than one.

Margaret and her team had also appeared from the dense fog, without warning and captured Zip adjusting himself. Before Barley, Bomber or Danny could react, the team had seized them and brought them to the ground.

'Slaps or thumps?' asked Margaret in a buoyant, victorious mood.

'Surrender,' replied Zip.

'I surrender as well,' chirped Bomber.

'And me, Margaret,' said Danny.

'Margaret, is it now?' she said sarcastically. 'No surrender,' she declared and thumped Zip three times on his head. The same treatment followed for Danny and then Bomber.

Barley, realising he was next on her agenda, struggled to break free but to no avail.

'Ah! Barley,' said Margaret, remembering with a satisfied smirk the last barney she had had with him, at her birthday party.

'Ah! Maggot,' he replied, in a defiant tone.

'How do you want it?' she asked. She showed her captive first a fist, and then the palm of her hand. 'Well, even grubs feed!'

'Well, it isn't three kisses I want, is it? Not from your bottom-of-the-ship-lips,' replied Barley.

Margaret slapped him twice on the head, thumped him twice more for good measure, then for good luck rapped his head with her knuckles. 'Have a headache, faceache,' said Margaret. She instructed her team to release their captives, who made their way sorrowfully to prison.

Chapter Two

'That's your chickens' problem in a nutshell, Bob,' said Barley, having streamlined the similarities between *his* chickens and the African ones. 'The cockerels are getting ready for a big massacre. It's up to you to ring a couple of chicken necks and give one to Danny and one to me, if you do that perhaps they'll get back to laying eggs in a normal fashion.'

Bob, of course, was tickled pink, by such a fascinating history of the fowl. 'Let's see how this week goes,' he said, lifting his cap and scratching his head. 'And, if you're right,' he went on to say, both thumbs again hooked in his waistcoat pocket, 'we'll know by Saturday morning.'

'We'll leave it till then, Bob,' replied Barley, sensing that his mission had already been accomplished. He then headed for the back gate and was soon off over the park to meet the boys for a pow-wow.

Barley ambled down the avenue, very pleased with himself. When he reached the terrace he noticed Porky, leaning against the fence outside his house, giving Bomber, Danny and Zip the evil eye.

Barley gave him a wide berth and slipped over to the other side of the avenue, turned right into the dead end by the railway lines and approached the boys from the footpath nearest the railway embankment, alongside the park instead.

Porky's reputation preceded him more than that of The Black Death. He was the only boy in school who enjoyed mashed potato and stew; the mashed potato was more like wallpaper paste and the stew poured like oil, drained from a lorry sump. That was no problem for Porky though and, providing the boys who were sat at his table pledged favours, he would eat their lunches as well. Word spread and soon every boy in school was falling over himself to sit at his table, promising him bigger and better favours. The jostling and pushing, just to sit down at Porky's table, eventually caused dissent, dissent that was of benefit to Porky. The boys who didn't keep their promises would be sat upon, until they screamed for mercy. Porky would then demand another favour. Though his larking about seemed innocent enough on the surface, it gradually evolved into a cynical game of intention when a few boys rallied round him and maliciously reinforced his demands. Porky found it to his liking and extorted much from the boys in school and on the estate. The camaraderie and harmless rivalry that existed between the various camps of boys was steering an ominous course with Porky at the helm.

Bomber, Danny and Zip were sprawled out on the grass, and hadn't seen Barley until they heard him say in a ghostly tone, 'Big Porky is watching yooou.' They sat up sharply, glanced over to the terrace, and let Barley elbow into position between them on the grass. 'How did it go?' inquired Danny, with one eye on Porky.

'All right,' replied Barley.

'Did Bob swallow it?' asked Danny.

'I think I convinced old Bob,' Barley said, with a winning smile.

'Think?' grimaced Danny. 'I hope you did.'

'Yes, of course I did. He was like putty in my hands.'

'What did you tell him?' asked Zip.

'A well-thought-out yarn. The sleep I lost working it out was something else, I can tell you,' said Barley. 'I was even up early this morning figuring out the last little details.'

'You gonna to tell us or what?' said Bomber, knowing Barley was beating around the bush.

Barley began to retell his tale of the domesticated chickens of deepest Africa and captivated the boys' imaginations...

'The professor leading the archaeological expedition was constipated and had just gone into the jungle to relieve himself. However, upon digging a hole, he stumbled upon a stone tablet, and decided to investigate the area further. Low and behold, to the professor's surprise, there were a host of similar tablets that, when pieced together, revealed the extraordinary story of the Humpit tribe. The tabloids, as the professor liked to call them in conversation, provided above all, a detailed description of the lifestyle of the tribe. Apparently, three tribes had co-existed in harmony for thousands of years: the Notsabarmy tribe, the Onyabike tribe and the Humpit tribe. From the information written on the tabloids, it seems that commerce between the tribes had flourished.

'The Humpit tribe thought of the chicken as sacred, and worshipped it in religious ceremonies. Huge statues of chickens, covered in feathers, were prominent on the top of totem poles throughout the village and the tribe bartered with chicken eggs.

'For the Humpit tribe, the fowl reigned supreme; members were forbidden, by law, to harm any of the birds, and those found breaking the law were duly punished and banished from Humping kingdom for ever. The Notsabarmy and Onyabike tribes, on the other hand, didn't involve themselves with such beliefs, and considered chicken meat delicious! Nevertheless, in honour of the

Humpit tribe, for its achievement in domesticating the wild fowl, the chiefs of the Notsabarmy and Onyabike tribes named the valley the Hump Plump valley.

'After deciphering many more tabloids, the professor discovered a more fascinating tale... One day chickens in the Humpit village hadn't laid any eggs for seven whole days. The chief of the Humpit tribe suspected foul play and blamed the Notsabarmy and Onyabike tribes, thinking that perhaps their witch doctors had cast spells over his entire village to prevent the chickens from laying eggs. He was convinced that they wanted his people to rid the village of the fowl, so it would become fair game for all.

'Meanwhile, the Notsabarmy and Onyabike chiefs believed that the Humpit tribe itself was deliberately withholding the eggs to push up their price. War drums beat out messages between the Notsabarmy and Onyabike tribes, resounding throughout the jungle, and panicked the Humpits into a state of frenzy. While Chief Humpit held a war council, his warriors built a defensive barrier encircling the village. By close of day, the blood-red sun had slipped down below the horizon, shedding its last light on the Humpit village. The camp fires crackled and flickered, shapeless shadows in the night, as the weird clucking sounds of chickens mingled with the noise of the jungle at night. It was that night however, that a mystical event happened that was to change the course of the tribe's culture for ever.

'First to awake the next morning was a young toddler called Izee. Rubbing his eyes as he yawned and stumbled from his hut into the village, he stopped and screamed in fright. Humpits in their hoards scampered from their huts in a panic. "Izee, Izee, control yourself," they shouted, booting his buttocks to try and shut him up.

'Then they realised why he had screamed so alarmingly. Never before had they seen such an awesome spectacle;

dead chickens lay scattered all around the village. Corpses lay by camp fires, oozing fat from charred skins, bodies were mutilated and orange flames hissed from charcoal carcasses. Amid the massacre, a few frightened chickens had jumped into a large pot of spices and been marinated to death.

'By far the most horrific sight could be seen beneath the mighty totem pole from which hung four young chicks, obviously in the prime of life, and who had clearly put up a brave fight before their lives had expired.

'The skin had been ripped from their bodies and their heads stuck up the parson's nose. Worst of all, was the sight of them skewered, left to roast over the hot embers. Villagers of all ages gazed in disbelief, acidic lumps choked their throats, as the chickens were gift-wrapped, in preparation for cremation.

'"Ooooohh," they spurned.

'One young warrior hurled himself forward, levelling his spear at the scene, shouting, "Notsabarmy!"

'"Onyabike!" shouted a second, leaping into the arena amid a cloud of settling dust from the first warrior.

'The witch doctor, realising that the Notsabarmy and Onyabike tribes couldn't possibly be responsible for the massacre, stepped forward and grasped the two warriors by the neck. "Oh, Humpit," he shouted, and explained why the Notsabarmy and Onyabike tribes could not have been responsible for the slaughter.

'"It was the cockerels that rebelled," said the witch doctor. "I, and I alone, will find the ultimate answer in the House of the Mighty Chicken Spirit."

'The chief instructed his drummers to begin communicating a declaration of peace and end to hostilities.

'The witch doctor's arduous task of reducing his intelligence to that of a chicken's, was, however, accomplished within seconds of his entering the Spirit House; he seemed to have much in common with the brain power of a chicken. In an upright, stiff position, he let his thoughts drift to the process of making eggs. Throughout that night the witch doctor mustered his thoughts together and put a spell on all the cockerels in the village.

'Morning came, and after what seemed a slight hesitation, the sun peaked over the treetops bringing both a fresh new dawn and the witch doctor's findings. He crawled away from the spirit house exhausted, on all fours, but feasted his eyes upon a wonderful sight. The cockerels had been busy all night in keeping with the witch doctor's spell, and the surviving chickens had produced eggs in little heaps outside every hut in the village. The witch doctor paid no heed to his own weakened body, instead ran around the village with glee. "Humpit, Humpit, Humpit."

'"Yes, yes, yes," replied the villagers.

'The chief summoned his people to a meeting so they might witness the witch doctor's wise judgement.

'Encircled by all the villagers, the witch doctor stood motionless, his chest puffed out proudly. Suddenly, he began to cluck, flap his arms as if they were wings, and strut, kicking up plumes of dust with one almighty, "Cock-a-Doodle-do."

'"It was the mighty cockerels who had slain the birds," he said, pointing his short stabbing spear at the throng of villagers.

'"They are hungry for fresh birds amongst their folds. They are no longer satisfied with old boilers, but desire fresh, young, juicy birds to carry out their bidding instead. Is it not proof of what I say that there are eggs a plenty this morning?" bid the witch doctor.

'The Humpit people nodded in agreement.

'"Then it is done. Upon the seventh day of no eggs, we must get rid of the old birds and replace them with fresh, young juicy ones," declared the witch doctor, pausing momentarily… "as for the old birds, we must hand them over to our Notsabarmy and Onyabike neighbours, as a goodwill gesture."

'And from that day forth, that procedure has been part of the tribe's culture to the present day,' Barley concluded.

Barley's account seemed plausible to Bomber and Danny, but Zip thought it would never fool Bob, let alone get him to part with two of his chickens.

'If old Bob swallows that one, you can cut my legs off and call me Shorty,' sniggered Zip. 'It's no wonder he didn't roll about laughing!'

Barley and Danny were surprised at Zip, for plenty of scheming and hard work was being put into their caper, and they believed their plan couldn't possibly fail.

'What does Bob know of African history?' said Danny. 'The eggs being collected will be put back at the weekend. That's surely more than enough to convince him… Course he'll swallow it, otherwise he would have said something straight away.'

'I reckon it'll work,' added Bomber, as a boost of confidence.

'I've no doubt,' said Barley, with a tinge of authority in his voice. 'When we're all sitting down, eating his chickens on Sunday, perhaps you'll believe us then?'

Zip disagreed in silence.

'We'll have to think of a good nickname for Danny – after all, it's him creeping round in the early hours,' added Barley.

'I don't want a nickname from all this caper,' said Danny, appalled himself at the idea. 'You're not calling me Embryo!' They all fell back onto the grass in fits of laughter.

'I can just hear it,' added Danny, fighting to keep a straight face, 'hello, this is me mate Embryo.'

They began larking around on the grass, unaware of the attention they were drawing to themselves.

Porky was heading in their direction, his beefy frame swaying from side to side. Bomber noticed Porky, gave the boys the whizz, and a calm mood once more prevailed. They sat upright and glanced around, adorned with false smiles.

'Watchya boys,' said Porky, expecting them to reciprocate the greeting, but they didn't. Instead they nodded their heads reservedly.

Porky barged into a space between them and squatted down, his fleshy stomach resting on both thighs and his shirt buttons stretched taut at the button holes. He looked at each boy in turn, and enquired, 'What you all laughing about?'

There was silence for a few seconds, then Bomber replied in a cool tone. 'How's it going?' Bomber then glanced at Porky's belly resting on his thighs, and remarked, 'Had your dinner yet, Porky?'

'Yep, lots of it,' Porky replied cheerfully, and patted his tummy.

'Looks like you've eaten you mother's as well,' said Barley, grinning.

Zip pointed to Porky's stout belly, 'Couldn't your dad eat his either?'

'Least ways won't get caught in me zip, Zip!' replied Porky, and laughed loudly at his own repartee.

Barley, Bomber and Danny gave no reaction to his sense of humour, in the hope he would soon feel unwelcome and depart as quickly as he had arrived but Zip was ready with an answer and just had to have the last word. 'Well, I don't know –' he said, 'If everything is in proportion to that fat gut of yours, you want to mind you don't get your head jammed in a door frame.'

Porky's repartee floundered and frustration showed on his face as he lunged forward. Zip's agile reaction was too fast; he rolled head over heels, jumped to his feet, and scampered out of harm's way, leaving Porky flat on his face.

'I'm warning you, Zip, I'll get you,' snarled Porky, and tried to regain his composure.

'Shut up, you lump of lard. Who are you kidding?' yelled Zip, mockingly.

'I'll kill him, I will, I'll kill him,' seethed Porky.

Zip was sat crossed-legged, watching from a safe distance, unable to hear what was being said. He realised something was afoot however, when he saw Porky begin to heckle the boys, unruffled by his tantrum. He raised his voice, wagged his finger, and then stormed off back towards the terrace. As Porky's distance increased from the parley, Zip's distance decreased until he was back sitting next to Barley.

'He took his time didn't he?' said Zip. 'What was he chin wagging about for so long.'

'You didn't help by winding him up,' replied Bomber accusingly.

'Wind him up! I'd like to string him up,' said Zip, and clenched his fists.

'We'd all like to do that,' said Bomber, raising his brow.

'Anyway...' said Zip, staring daggers at Porky on the terrace.

'What did he want?'

'Bragging, as usual,' yawned Danny.

'About his latest escapade,' added Barley.

'What's he gonna do then?' Zip asked.

'...What I didn't like,' said Bomber, thrusting his forefinger hard onto the grass, 'was the way Porky, more or less told us we'd better go and see his escapade tonight, or else.'

'He was threatening us all right,' confirmed Barley.

'Look,' said Danny, attempting to put the situation into perspective. 'Take no notice, he's all mouth and trousers.'

Bomber tore up a handful of grass and threw it into Danny's face, and the boys carried on larking about.

Porky and his crew had gathered, just before dusk, outside his house on the terrace green and from there they headed along the terrace, crossed the avenue, and entered the dead end by the railway lines. Bomber alerted the boys when he saw Porky wave for them to join his crew on the terrace, but they took no notice.

Porky was an awkward climber, so his crew adopted a pecking order. Porky was first over the railings onto the embankment. When the crew had scaled the spiked railings, Porky again beckoned Barley, Bomber, Danny and Zip to join him. They made out to be unaware of this, but Porky's demanding threats, echoing across the park, eventually compelled them to attend his latest show of bravado.

The gradient of the embankment formed a ditch behind the boundary fences of back gardens. Kids on the estate had trodden a snaking path near the fence, for shortcuts over the railway lines and easy access to the open fields and rural expanse. The families living in the area paid little attention to kids running over the railway lines; the majority had children who, at sometime or other, had erected camps in the ditch or taken shortcuts over the railway lines themselves. It was a common occurrence to see kids messing about on the railway lines.

Porky wanted to impress on all the boys living on the estate, that he was daring and willing to take risks. Gathering his audience against the boundary fencing of the lower embankment, he stood on the opposite embankment, and let loose a stream of verbal diarrhoea of courage!

'How many of you think I won't do it?' he asked, slowly pacing back and forth.

His audience didn't murmur a word.

'Who's gonna do it, if I do?' he said cockily.

One third of the boys all shook their heads, the remainder shrugged their shoulders, content to witness his stunt. Porky removed his jacket, tucked the bottom of his trousers in his socks and tightened his belt. His composure was calm, and with both hands on his hips, he stood peering down at his audience. The signalling cables twanged and squeaked on their rollers attached to the small concrete posts beside the railway and the track lines began to vibrate.

Porky glanced up the railway track at an approaching train, punching out smoke to a speedy chorus of clattering wheels. As the mobile maiden forged ahead with rumbling shock waves, its whistle blew twice, and the shuddering of earth gained momentum.

Porky stepped out over the signalling cables, to stand between the railway lines, facing the oncoming train. Not giving way to panic, he lay spread eagle on the sleepers, slipped both hands and feet under the railway lines, and with his face on the chipped granite, lay in wait for the train to roar overhead. The audience gazed awe-struck as the train chugged over Porky with a deafening crescendo of noise. Eventually, the juddering clanks of steel wheels on jointed railway tracks gradually diminished and the guard's van finally rolled past.

Porky stood up and punched his fists into the air. With his chest out proudly, and his ego duly expanded, he shook his fists as a boxer would, having won twelve bouts. Expecting some praises of, 'Well Done' and Porky was appeased with some low voiced compliments as he stepped over the signalling cables.

'Beat that, if you can!' he said, thinking he was the epitome of bravery. Porky slipped his jacket on calmly, then slid down the embankment to the bottom of the ditch, and looked up at his audience with a smug smile.

Barley, stood next to Bomber, murmured, 'He's raving bonkers.'

'You can say that again,' replied Bomber, behind a cupped hand.

Porky's big mouthed and full of wind – and his stunt didn't impress me, thought Danny, and in a flash of inspiration, he felt an irresistible urge to throw down a challenge himself. Grabbing the opportunity by the scruff of its neck, Danny pushed himself forward.

'What you did was nothing, Porky,' he blurted, leaning against the fence ready for a quarrel. 'Anyone can just lie down under a train. You've just got to be thick, that's all,' continued Danny dismissing Porky's efforts with a wave of his hand. Every boy there was dumbfounded.

Porky, still at the bottom of the ditch, glared at Danny with a reddening face. 'I'd like to see you do it, Mighty Mouth,' he shouted.

'I'm better than that,' replied Danny and grinned. 'I don't have a thick head and torso like you, that's for sure.' Danny realised that there was no going back on his challenge now, and that the same applied for Porky, left with no other choice but take up the challenge, or lose face in front of his crew. Porky certainly wasn't about to do that.

'How are you gonna top that, Mouthpiece?' growled Porky.

Danny felt exhilarated by his own confidence and a broad, cheeky smile eased across his face as he gazed down at the enraged Porky. 'Getting worried, are you?' mocked Danny.

'Oh yeah,' sneered Porky. 'You do it, and I'll do it better.' Porky scrambled up the embankment adjacent to his crew, held onto the fence with one hand, and waited for Danny's reply.

'…All right then,' said Danny, after a moment of silence.

'Tomorrow night... meet you on the footbridge, an hour earlier than tonight and we'll see how clever you are.'

'No problem, Mouthpiece,' said Porky, and pointed a finger at Danny. 'So what is it you reckon on doing then?'

'Losing your bottle?' said Danny, and smirked.

'Don't worry, I'll be there,' snapped Porky.

'I dunno?' goaded Danny.

'You just try and stop me, Mouthpiece,' Porky replied, spitefully.

'Oh, I won't,' said Danny, feeling content in the knowledge that Porky had accepted a challenge without knowing any of the details.

Instead of backtracking to the spiked railings, Bomber led the way along the embankment ridge to his back garden, over the fence, down the garden into the alley, and out in to the avenue for a pow-wow. They sat cross-legged beneath the dim light of the gas lamp, and as Danny began revealing what was up his sleeve, the three boys listened with pricked ears.

'Did you see the way Porky climbed over the railings?' said Danny.

The trio of heads nodded in agreement.

'He's oversize, clumsy, and has no sense of timing whatsoever. There's no doubt in my mind. I'm more agile than he'll ever be and that's where I have the advantage. I've watched his capers for a long time; he always picks on the vulnerable, boys who aren't capable of standing up for themselves. Tonight's escapade was no different. He wanted to impress and consolidate his image as a rough diamond. In actual fact it was nothing,' said Danny. 'The train was a relatively slow goods train; they always roll along at a leisurely pace. Despite their rumbling noise and impressive image, all Porky had to do was keep very still. It would have been a different story if it was an express train; there's a possibility of being sucked up into the vacuum and cut to shreds. My stunt on the other hand will involve split timing, good judgement and the ability to keep one's balance. Porky'll be the laughing stock of school, and the estate... But I'll need you three to help me,' said Danny.

'How do we fit in then?' asked Zip.

Danny smiled, knowing if Zip took the bait, so would Barley and Bomber. 'Barley, has your old man still got that tarpaulin sheet stuck to the top of his shed?'

'Yeah, he has,' replied Barley.

'Can you get hold of it for me?'

'You'll have to help me carry it,' Barley replied, and stuck both thumbs up for an affirmative yes.

'Good,' said Danny, 'the sheet is the main thing. Bomber, can you get hold of six long batons, like those your old man keeps in the garden, and Zip can you get some rope, not too thick but strong all the same.'

'Not a problem,' replied both Bomber and Zip.

'Whatever happens – we've got to keep this hush-hush,' said Danny. 'We'll have to do this in complete secrecy... I tell you now, Porky's in for a big shock tomorrow night!'

Chapter Three

Barley arrived home from school the next day and set about trying to persuade his father that he needed the tarpaulin sheet for the end of term school play. '…To use it as a Bedouin tent dad,' Barley explained and was granted.

Zip, thinking his task would be the easiest, searched high and low in the garden shed for a length of rope but could only find a piece of string. Not wanting to be beaten, he decided to borrow next door's washing line; there was no washing hanging on the line, and it appeared to be the obvious solution. By the time his neighbour realised it was missing, he'd be long gone. Anyway, thought Zip, who would know it was me that borrowed the washing line? There was, however, a problem with this idea: his next door neighbour was busy hand-washing in the sink by the window that looked out into the back garden. To get round this, Zip sauntered over to his younger sister, playing near the garden gate, and knelt down on one leg next to her. 'Shall we play a lovely ball game, Shirley?'

Shirley looked at her brother with big innocent eyes, overjoyed; it wasn't often he noticed her, let alone play games with her. She agreed wholeheartedly.

Zip cracked a smile the width of the Cheshire cat, fetched his football from the shed and ushered Shirley into the front garden. He positioned her by next door's fence, then artfully lobbed the ball into his neighbour's front garden.

'Oh! Shirley,' he said, in mock surprise. 'You didn't catch it did you? You'll have to go and fetch the ball.' Zip opened the front gate and watched Shirley knock on the neighbour's front door to ask permission to retrieve the ball. Zip ran faster than a rocket, round the back garden and penknife at the ready, he peeked out from behind the shed. When he saw that the coast was clear, he leapt over the garden fence, cut down the washing line threw the line over into his garden, wrapped the washing line around his waist, and rejoined Shirley.

'I don't want to play any more,' pouted Zip. 'You play on your own,' and shoved Shirley into the back garden.

Barley and Danny struggled with the tarpaulin sheet every inch of the way to Bomber's house. However, when they reached the bottom of the alleyway and leaned against the back gate for a breather, it opened suddenly. Both boys fell to the ground, tarpaulin in between them.

Bill stood towering over them, his beady eyes scanning down the thin ridge of his hooked nose. His mouth opened exposing his toothless gums, and he spluttered, 'Where do you think you're going with that?'

'Where's your broomstick, Bill?' said Danny, and chuckled.

'You cheeky young git,' replied Bill, and pushed his cap back on his head.

'It's all right, Dad,' shouted Bomber, from the bottom of the garden. 'We're crossing the railway lines with it.'

Bill glanced up, gave a nod of approval, went back into the house and thought no more of the matter.

Zip suggested they tie the batons together to make a rack for the tarpaulin sheet, 'to share the weight equally between the four of us,' he said, and took charge of its fabrication.

After checking all directions for railway police, the boys climbed over the fence, skidded down the embankment, scurried up the bank, crossed the railway lines, and then down the embankment to the ditch on the other side.

Zip wanted to check out the mousetraps he had previously set in the fields, before going any further. Having spent a fair amount of time making them for the prank he intended to pull on the Bughutch, he wasn't about to be dissuaded. Although the boys had willingly offered to help in the trap's construction, knowing none of them had the patience or the skill to help, Zip had refused their offer. Besides, he wanted to take full credit for all the intended results.

Zip wasn't gone long, for he soon returned to the embankment with a couple of pre-trapped mice. The boys then began traipsing along the bottom of the ditch towards the footbridge. The overgrown bracken made their passage difficult, nor did it inspire a vision of great accomplishment. They struggled on regardless, until they had reached a suitable spot, opposite Zip's back garden and flopped down in exhaustion.

'Phew! I'm glad of a breather,' said Barley, and wiped his brow.

'Not many,' agreed Bomber.

'*Think* of me guys,' said Zip, and scrambled up the embankment to the railway lines.

Danny had explained that it was necessary to haul the tarpaulin into the opposite ditch, for if Porky was in the park or on the terrace he would surely see them, and their game would be foiled. The boys had grasped the drift of Danny's plan, but niggling in the back of Bomber's mind, was the problem of how to conceal a dirty great tarpaulin sheet from Porky's view once erected. He posed the question.

'Simple,' replied Danny. 'I've always noticed one thing when I was train spotting from the footbridge you lot ever did.'

'What?' asked Bomber.

'Trust me for now. I'll surprise you later with how simple it is.' Zip came back over the railway lines, down the grassy bank and joined them.

'There's a load of mice now,' he panted. 'Twenty or more.'

'Great stuff,' said Danny, and jumped to his feet.

'No rest for me then,' said Zip, lying flat on his back.

'Time *is* getting on,' replied Danny, and grabbed a corner of the rack.

Danny thought that skirting the footbridge to the other side would prove to be the hardest obstacle. He hadn't, however, reckoned on hauling the tarpaulin through stagnant water and long grass clinging to every piece of junk, making their journey difficult. With scratched hands beginning to blister, wet feet, and aching backs, they fell onto the embankment near the footbridge, totally exhausted.

Danny felt assured his contrivance would work but the boys were starting to think the whole idea utter nonsense.

'Just a bit further,' urged Danny, 'and we'll be at the footbridge.'

'You sure this plan of yours is going to work?' said Zip.

'I'm positive,' replied Danny.

'Well, tell us how,' Zip said, in a critical tone.

Danny was aware that the boys needed some inspiration and so lifted their spirits with a verbal scenario of Porky's forthcoming downfall that night. Then, without warning, an express train raced past them, shaking the ground with an ear splitting din, bringing them jolting back to the reality of the task in hand. Furtively, they scooted round the footbridge, down the embankment and along the ditch on the other side.

'That's far enough,' said Danny, and the boys let the tarpaulin drop like a lead weight.

With the stealth of tigers, they crept up the grassy embankment to the brow of the hill, popped their heads over the ridge and surveyed the location to the other side of the railway lines. Barley, Bomber and Zip were without a clue as to what they were supposed to be looking at, but gave the thumbs up sign anyway.

'Now do you see?' said Danny, pointing a finger at a yellow brick wall on the other side. 'Porky will never see it.'

The three boys nodded their heads in agreement, yet still asked, 'See what?'

'You're unreal,' said Danny, and slumped his head in his hands. With a deep breath he replied, 'Cast your eyes to the footbridge, follow the railway lines and you'll see it spans over the cut. You see the high, yellow brick wall of the coal yard? If you follow the wall towards the station, it ends where the houses start. Right?'

The three boys again gave a nod of agreement.

'Now, what do you see in the middle of the brick wall?' asked Danny.

'Bricks,' replied Zip.

'Well, I know that,' said Danny.

'It cuts back in the middle and runs along until it reaches the houses,' said Bomber.

'That's right,' confirmed Danny, pleased that one of the boys was finally enlightened. 'That's where I want to erect the tarpaulin sheet. Right in the corner of that recess.'

'Porky will see it, and he'll want the same advantage as you,' snapped Zip.

'That's where you're wrong,' replied Danny. 'If we erect the sheet tight in the corner of the recess, he won't see it from the footbridge. Look how many times we've been over that bridge – none of you've ever noticed the recess. What Porky will see is the same as you. When I've finished the stunt, I'll cut the tarpaulin sheet down and camouflage it.'

'What if it don't work and Porky don't lose face?' remarked Bomber.

'Come off it,' said Danny. 'You take it from me, he'll lose face all right. It's goodbye Porky.'

Before darting across the railway lines, the boys made sure that there were no trains approaching from either way, there were no pedestrians crossing the footbridge and that passengers, waiting on the station platform weren't looking.

Working fast, they positioned the batons transversely below the brow of the embankment but above the bottom of the ditch, spread the tarpaulin sheet lengthways over the batons and secured the corner with the washing line. They then bound the edges of the tarpaulin sheet to the batons, cleared all the debris from under the sheet and set about collecting a heap of grass for camouflage.

Danny knew it was his neck on the line should this fail and doubled checked beneath the sheet to make sure it was taut and securely fixed.

'Well,' said Bomber, parking his backside on the grass next to the boys, 'that's about it.'

'That's perfect,' replied Danny, glancing up at the sheet.

'Least the bottom of this ditch isn't wet like the other side,' said Zip, looking at his sodden feet.

'My feet are soaking too,' confirmed Barley.

'We'd better get a move on then,' said Danny.

So the boys backtracked to Bomber's house, arriving in plenty of time for dinner.

Chapter Four

Porky and the biggest member of his crew (Bacon) played
football against three other crew members: they made do
with two empty milk bottle crates for goal posts, and both
teams played towards the same goalkeeper. As they dribbled
and squabbled for possession of the leather ball, Porky
barged the opposing team out of his way and kicked the
ball, square to his outside right to Bacon, then ran towards
the goalposts shouting for Bacon to play the ball back to
him. Bacon kicked a long ball diagonally to Porky, who
gave it an almighty kick, over the keeper's head.

'Goal! Goal!' Porky bellowed and ran back up the pitch
in a frenzy of ecstatic delight, expecting a pat on the back
from Bacon. The keeper, however, protested that the ball
had gone over the imaginary bar.

'That was miles too high,' the keeper shouted and indicated to the bar above. 'Miles too high.'

Porky scowled in disbelief and headed back up the pitch
to settle the difference of opinion.

'That was not a goal, and you know it,' snarled the
keeper.

'That *was* a goal,' growled Porky, infuriated.

'No it wasn't, anyone could see that,' said the keeper,
looking to the other players to confirm his opinion. But,
they remained tight-lipped and rooted to the spot.

Porky came to a halt in front of the keeper and stood
with legs apart and his arms folded across his chest. 'That

was a goal,' he said, with a piercing glare. 'Wasn't it?' he said, and his arms dropped to his side.

'No it wasn't,' replied the keeper defiantly, and placed both hands on his hips.

Without warning, Porky pounced on the keeper and pulled him close. 'That *was* a goal, wasn't it?' asked Porky again, then stepped on the keeper's foot, pressing down hard. 'Wasn't it?' repeated Porky, violently trying to shake the defiance out of the keeper.

'Yes, yes. It *was* a goal, Porky,' replied the keeper, his chin puckered in fright.

Porky pushed the keeper backwards, tripped him to the ground and pointed at him. 'You'd better watch it in future, or else,' he warned, turned and marched back up the pitch.

When the keeper had recovered, he fetched the football and then spotted Danny, Barley, Bomber and Zip heading in his direction.

Danny was feeling unnerved at having witnessed Porky's sense of justice and kept a discreet eye on the crew gathering round Porky in support.

'I've got butterflies now, boys,' muttered Danny.

'Don't let them flutter in your head,' muttered Bomber out of the corner of his mouth.

Porky sat down on a milk crate, and his crew stood behind him in semi-circular fashion.

Danny, Barley and Bomber halted and stood facing the opposition, while Zip hovered in the background. The bold, abusive stares exchanged between both groups charged a tense silence for a few moments, and then the silence was broken. 'So, what's this big dare then?' said Porky. 'Are we going to see something out of this world?'

The crew pointed at Danny and chuckled derisively. Danny's heart pounded faster, but his face was expressionless, and he gave a wry grin.

'Let me put it this way, Porky,' said Danny. 'It'll start off in *this* world but it might end up in another one for *you*.'

'So, what *is* the dare, you clown?' sneered Porky.

'Your bottle going already, boy?' blurted Bomber and stepped forward.

'Up yours,' was Porky's reply and raised his brow.

'I would, but it isn't as big as yours, is it?' growled Bomber.

'Do you want it now?' threatened Porky and showed his fist.

'If you like,' barked Bomber.

Porky was up and off the milk crate in a flash, his fists at the ready, before Danny barged between them.

'We gonna get on with it or what?' said Danny, being buffeted between the two boys.

'Suits me fine,' replied Porky, still squaring up to Bomber. 'So what *is* the dare?'

'I'll tell you… if you two back off,' said Danny, and the pair backed away from each other.

Danny steered Porky away from his crew and towards the footbridge, explaining his dare loud enough so that the crew could hear for themselves. He also expected his rival to react with an avalanche of fear and uncertainty at his audacious dare. But, Danny was taken aback when Porky seemed oblivious to any danger and instead threw a spanner in the works by suggesting that he perform the dare first.

'No, no, no,' protested Danny, as his thoughts froze for a moment. '…It's my idea,' he added and waited for Porky's reaction.

'It's up to you. It don't bother me,' replied Porky, shrugging his shoulders. 'There's nothing to it.'

Danny's confidence was shaken with self doubt; he wondered whether his flash of inspirational bravado had overshadowed his common sense. Graphic fears of events furrowed his imagination: the breaking of both his legs, or worse, fracturing his spine and being crippled for life. He even thought of the ultimate, Death.

The convoy of boys reached the footbridge and Danny was first to tread the first two tiers of steps. The third tier was at a ninety degree angle and led to the gangway over the railway lines. Danny's heart beat rapidly, his mouth was dried out, cold shivers tingled up his spine and his thoughts rattled around like jumping beans in a empty drum. Then Bomber's words sprang to mind. 'Don't let the butterflies into your head.' That's easier said than done, thought Danny and struggled to quash his doubting notions.

Both groups of boys bulked like lemmings onto the centre of the gangway, and Bomber suggested they take up positions on either side, on the steps. This was in order that they could still see clearly from behind the steel lattice railings and that it wouldn't bring attention to themselves from passers-by.

Porky and Danny stood together. Bomber, Barley and Zip stood close on the gangway.

Danny discreetly glanced over to the recess in the yellow brick wall, but it could not be seen. Great, he thought.

Familiar with the train timetable, Danny knew that a goods train would be along shortly, and then it would be the point of no return.

'I can see one,' said Barley excitedly.

Danny crossed over to the other side of the gangway and focused his gaze on the oncoming train to judge its speed. It's an empty coal train all right, thought Danny, and it's rolling along steady enough. Just as well, as if the train was travelling too fast, it would be impossible to jump.

Porky, leaning on the lattice railings with both hands in his pockets, sniggered, 'Huh! Nothing to it.'

Bomber glared at Porky in distaste. 'You'll find out soon enough, won't you?' he said as the train blew its whistle.

Danny rushed back over to the other side of the gang-way and began climbing the railings. He was assertive with every step and made the ascent look as though he were an expert. He clambered over the spiky counter-rail, was soon astride the obelisk capping and then descended safely onto the smoke-guard jutting out over the railway line.

Every boy had his face tight against the railings to catch a glimpse of the dare-devil in action.

The train bellowed out smoke, hissed steam and chugged under the footbridge with a frightening clatter. Danny held on tight to the railings in the swirling haze of smoke. As the choking haze slowly evaporated, he shuffled to the edge of the smoke-guard. His timing was exact, and he made a spectacular leap into the back of an empty coal truck. Shouts rang out from all the boys, and they scampered up the steps to the centre of the footbridge, gathered in captivated silence.

Barley let out a yell, 'Yes he's all right.'

Danny was covered in coal dust, and could be seen scrambling up the sides of the coal truck as it swayed with the momentum, both legs astride on the corners. He stood up with arms outstretched for balance and, as the coal truck neared the tarpaulin sheet in the recess, he leapt across with the deftness of a black panther, amid deafening cheers and thumping feet echoing from the footbridge.

Danny had no time to waste. He wriggled off the tarpaulin at one end, cut the washing line and then pulled down the batons. Gathering his safety net into the bottom of the ditch, first reducing its bulk by stamping it down, he then camouflaged the sheet with the heap of pre-prepared grass.

Meanwhile, on the footbridge, Porky wasn't at all impressed by Danny's performance. 'That's nothing. I don't know what all the fuss is about,' he said in a disgruntled tone. 'You sound like a bunch of demented loonies cheering like that, if you ask me.'

'No one *did* ask you,' retorted Bomber.

Danny emerged from the recess, brushing coal-dust off his clothes as roaring cheers rang out from his audience. Then he sprinted along the track, back under the footbridge and scaled the boundary fence into the park, to be congratulated by all the boys. Porky stood at the back of the group, locked out of the fun by his calumny. Smarting, Porky glared daggers of resentment at Danny and realised only too well that he would find it hard to emulate such a polished performance. Danny broke through the ring of boys surrounding him and stood in front of Porky. 'Your turn next,' he challenged.

'I could do it on me head,' laughed Porky.

'We'll see when the next coal train comes, won't we?' sniped Danny.

'Oh, you will,' replied Porky, in a tone of sour grapes, and took command of his crew. 'Right, you lot, we'll have a kick about in the park while we're waiting for the next train.'

That's good, thought Danny, for he didn't want to fraternise with his opponent any more than necessary. Besides, he wanted to chinwag with the boys; he could hardly do that with the opposition within hearing distance.

'Did you camouflage the tarpaulin sheet?' asked Bomber, as they sat on the steps of the footbridge.

'He'll never see it,' replied Danny and glanced over at Porky from behind the lattice railings. 'That's if he ever gets on the train.'

'How was your landing in the coal truck?' asked Zip.

'Not too bad. I rolled and hit the back of the truck. The hardest bit was keeping me balance just before jumping off. I tell you now, boys, Porky isn't going to jump off that coal truck,' said Danny. 'He'll be too scared, that's why. So where will he end up? I tell you where he'll end up, somewhere up the country. The beauty of it is... we get to wave him goodbye in front of all his cronies.'

'Can you see it?' said Barley. 'It'll be midnight when Porky gets off the train in the middle of nowhere, looks about and sees a guard; he'll go running up to him, "Mr, Mr, they played a dirty trick on me and I can't get home", and the guard'll say, "I can see why an' all, you need a good wash".'

The boys chuckled and Bomber gave his preview of events that might take place that night.

'No, I'll tell you what will happen. The train will stop in some goods yard, patrolled by guards with Alsatians. Porky creeps out of the coal truck and thinks the coast is clear, he starts running for it and the guard spots him and lets the guard dog loose. This great, growling Alsatian then runs after Porky and bites a chunk out of his meaty bum!'

'Which will happen if there's any justice,' said Zip, wanting to give his version.

'When Porky jumps onto the train, he'll bump his head and knock himself unconscious and lose his memory. The railway police will find him and hand him over to some hospital for misfits. When he regains consciousness, the hospital realises he's lost his memory. After some research, the authorities are unable to find where the "freak" originates from, so they decide it's time to operate and open up his brain. To their amazement, it's frog's spawn he's got for brains! One doctor turns to the other and says, "How can this be? How does he think?" Then the other doctor replies, "I don't know but it would account for him hopping on a train".'

Almost an hour had passed before the next coal train was spotted. Danny was fast on to his feet and was checking whether it was indeed a coal carrier. 'That's it,' he said and clapped his hands.

'Here comes your joy ride, Porky,' he yelled, with his face tight against the lattice railings.

'It's about time,' bellowed Porky, turned and headed for the footbridge.

Everyone quickly returned to their previous spectator's positions on the footbridge. Barley noticed that Porky's face was ashen. He noted too, when the train blew its whistle, that Porky's breathing was deeper, and that he was showing signs of anxiety.

'Come on, it's getting nearer. Hurry up,' said Danny, with great delight.

Porky began climbing the railings. A sheen of perspiration glossed his face close to his hairline and fine beads of sweat trickled down to his ear lobes. Clambering over the spiky ridge, he clung on tightly with every foot of descent. When he was firmly on the smoke-guard, he shuffled around and leaned over to look down at the railway lines. Black smoke from the train's funnel billowed in his face. Stunned, Porky's thoughts were fragmented, and he lurched backwards and grabbed the railings, holding on for dear life. Sensing everyone's gaze upon him, waiting for his next move, he turned around slowly again to face the empty coal trucks. He shuffled to the edge of the smoke-guard and stood nervously gazing down, unsure whether to jump or to lose face.

'Jump, why don't you?' shouted Bomber. The words peeved Porky, and he jumped.

'Farewell, blossom,' shouted Danny.

Porky's crew scurried up the steps to the gangway, jostling for a better view.

'That's him off up the road,' chuckled Zip and looked to Bomber.

The coal trucks rolled up the railway line towards the station, and there was no sign of Porky.

'With his body mass,' said Zip, 'I hope he's not crashed through the bottom of the truck.'

'There he is,' said Danny, and pointed through the railings, in utter surprise.

Clear enough, for all to see, Porky's head popped up in the corner of the coal truck.

'Hooray,' shouted his crew.

Porky struggled up the sides and managed to kneel on his shins astride the corner. He then manoeuvred his feet onto the sides of the truck and held on tightly.

Porky straightened his legs and was bent over, holding on with both hands.

'He's never going to jump,' said Bomber, in dismay.

'He is,' replied Danny, feeling gutted.

'He'll break his back,' said Zip. 'With any luck he will anyway.'

Bent over like a gorilla on a treelimb, with little time before the train reached the station platform, Porky stood up and leapt clear from the coal truck into the ditch. Danny felt a demoralised wave of despair sweep over him. 'He's got to have broken some bones,' he said and wished the worse.

'Let's hope he has,' replied Barley.

'I can't hear any cries of agonising pain. I mean you would have heard the cries, even from this distance,' said Bomber.

'Of course you would have; you would have heard screams and squeals, as you would from pigs,' said Zip.

They couldn't believe their eyes: Porky came crawling over the brow of the embankment, and they could see how he'd managed to land to safety, he was dripping wet, from head to toe and smothered in green algae.

The spectators laughed scornfully, as the sodden stunt man squelched towards the bridge. The laughter from the footbridge was relentless, and it fuelled Porky's anger to the limit. Then suddenly, his soggy trundle was halted by the recess in the yellow brick wall. Something had caught his attention, and he went striding over for a closer inspection.

'That wasn't suppose to happen,' laughed Danny, holding his sides. 'But now that it has…'

'And neither was *that* suppose to happen,' said Barley, and indicated at Porky, pulling and tugging at the tarpaulin sheet like a demented bull terrier with a piece of cloth between his teeth.

Porky was unable to pull the tarpaulin sheet completely clear of the ditch for his crew to see the contrivance, and his face turned purple with red rage. 'Get hold of them. Get them!' he ranted, at the top of his voice and broke into a squelchy sprint.

Porky's crew rushed towards the boys and a huge, entangled, wrestling match ensued.

Barley and Danny were the first to escape from the fracas, quickly followed by both Bomber and Zip.

They fled like rabbits pursued by greyhounds, across the park to Bell Lane, to the safety of the Avenue. They looked back over the park and could just see the faint outline of Porky and crew, heading in their direction.

'I thought the bottom of that ditch was dry?' said Zip, catching his breath. 'I bet you the young kids in those houses built a dam.'

'It could only have been that,' said Barley. 'We've done the same ourselves.'

'That's a good a bet as any,' said Danny.

'So,' said Bomber, having caught his breath, 'We'll get Porky next time.'

'Next time?' the boys exclaimed in surprise.

'You don't think Porky is going to leave it there? We escaped from him tonight but there's school tomorrow, and he'll be looking for revenge.'

They agreed that after the night's fiasco, gloves would be off. They glanced over the park again and saw Porky waving his fist and shouting abuse at them.

'We'll have to recover the tarpaulin sheet tomorrow night,' said Barley. 'If that goes missing, me dad will kill me.'

'I'll be worn-out in the morning,' said Danny. 'I'm collecting chicken eggs at daylight, don't forget.'

'I'll give you a hand, if yer like,' replied Barley.

'Porky's getting too close for comfort,' said Zip. 'I say we make a move now.'

'Don't worry too much,' said Bomber. 'The Drip has to dry off first.'

The next morning, Porky's crew gathered on the terrace outside Porky's house, waiting to catch the other boys on their way to school.

Bomber, guessing Porky's intentions, suggested that they gather behind the close-boarded fence of the end terrace house, opposite Zip's house, and scout the Terrace. Danny lay flat on his tummy, wiggled forward, and peeked round the corner. 'He's there and looking this way.'

'Did he spot you?' asked Zip anxiously.

'No chance,' replied Danny, brushing the dust from his clothes.

'It's what we expected,' said Barley.

'Let's have it out with them, here and now,' said Bomber angrily. 'We were unprepared last night for a brawl. Let's give them what for, now.'

Danny, Barley and Zip didn't think much of that idea, and pointed out they were out-numbered. Besides, between the four of them, no one was capable of matching Porky, and his side kick Bacon. Perhaps without those two, it would be an even match but it wasn't a sure bet.

'But what is a sure bet?' said Danny. 'Porky's regular habits. He'll be doing his rounds of extortion – he's not going to be late for that is he.'

'You've got it right there, Danny,' said Bomber. So, they stayed put behind the fence, waited for Porky to make a move towards the school, and decided to cycle to school the long way round, through the allotments.

'Great,' said Barley. 'I've got a puncture.'

'Jump on me cross-bar,' suggested Bomber, and they went off to collect their bicycles.

The allotments had been abandoned since before the Second World War. The local authorities intended to develop the land for sporting activities and connect it to the school but that was put on a back burner for a later date, owing to the lack of finances. In the meantime, every kid on the estate had used the allotments for games of all descriptions: supposed secret camps littered the site, dirt tracks were used for scrambling games and shortcuts in all directions were used by all, day and night. The vegetation had reclaimed the neglected plots but they were still distinguishable by the bushy tufts of grass growing around their perimeters.

The boys halted their bikes on the edge of the ash road that weaved its way through the allotments and could see the school entrance through the gaps in the evergreen hedgerow on the far side. There was no sign of Porky outside the gates but they still watched the last of the pupils going into the school before making a move to cycle across the allotments. Zip and Danny set off across the allotments, kicking up plumes of dust in their wake.

'Trust us to cop all the dust,' said Barley, fanning the dust from his face.

'Should have mended your puncture then,' replied Bomber with a grin.

The bike shook violently, and Barley tried easing the jolts by lifting one side of his bum off the cross bar. 'Slow down on the bumps,' he complained.

'Don't think about the bumps. It's all in your mind,' said Bomber and deliberately drove into a big rut.

'Ouch! I can't help it,' groaned Barley.

'I forgot,' said Bomber, 'your brains are in your bum!' and chuckled with delight, steering straight for another rut.

'Huh,' moaned Barley, 'at this rate my brains will fall out.'

Zip and Danny had gained a fair distance in front of Barley and Bomber when suddenly they came to a screeching halt. They dismounted their bikes and sauntered over to a young boy, sitting with his head in his hands, on a grassy knoll near the hawthorn hedgerow. His school blazer had chalk daubed all over it, and he looked as if he'd been dragged through the dusty undergrowth. Close by, was his satchel lying open, books, pencils and papers ripped and strewn all over. His lunch box had been tossed into the hedgerow and his sandwiches trampled upon. When the young boy glanced up and saw Zip and Danny approaching, he feared the worse and started to cry. Zip crouched down, and asked what had happened. The boy snivelled and rubbed his eyes with the back of his hands, reluctant to answer. Then Barley and Bomber came over and they all gathered round.

'This is Porky's doing,' declared Barley.

The young boy sniffled, wiped his eyes and confirmed Barley's guess with a nod of his head.

'He's a dirt bag,' said Barley.

The boys glanced up at each other with undeniable repulsion and knew Porky's reasoning only too well: unable to lay his hands on them, he had vented his frustration out on the first boy he had came across.

'Haven't you a handkerchief in your pocket?' asked Bomber.

'No,' sobbed the boy.

Bomber pulled a rag handkerchief from his pocket and handed it to him. 'What's your name?' asked Bomber.

'Stuart,' he replied and sobbed. 'They held me down, searched me and took my pocket money,' he wept.

Danny crouched and placed his hand on Stuart's shoulder. 'Don't worry, Stuart,' said Danny. 'We'll help you collect your gear.'

Zip gathered up the textbooks, pencils and papers, tucked them in the satchel, and the boys brushed the chalk marks off Stuart's blazer.

'Is this the first time Porky's picked on you?' asked Barley.

Stuart frowned, not wanting to answer but after some encouragement from Barley, he was persuaded.

'Yes, yes, it is,' Stuart floundered. 'Although he did call me Dopey in the playground on several occasions but that's all really.'

'What made him call you Dopey?' asked Danny.

'It started with PE lessons. I was having trouble jumping over the horse, and Mr Fielding started saying, "hurry up, Dopey". Later I was in the playground, a few of the boys started larking about and called me Dopey. The big stout boy heard, and started calling me Dopey too.'

'You're in the first year aren't you, Stuart?' said Danny.

'Yes,' replied Stuart. 'I'm in Cook House.'

With eight houses in the school class system, Stuart was in the top notch house.

'That's just as well,' said Danny. 'Porky and three of his gang are in our house, the other two are in Hudson.'

The boys picked up their bikes and sauntered from the allotments, across Bell Lane and into school.

The cycle racks were full, so they left their bicycles leaning against the walls of the prefab classrooms adjacent to the playground. Now that Stuart was a casualty of Porky, the boys knew he would be prone to future harassment. Bomber and Danny advised Stuart to report the incident to his Housemaster, Mr James.

'Don't be afraid to be called a grass. That's what Porky counts on… you not saying a word… it gives him the edge,' said Danny, and promised to back up his complaint.

'Don't you worry, Stuart,' said Bomber. 'I'm going to report the matter to our Housemaster, Mr Barret.'

Before going their separate ways to registration, Bomber arranged to meet Stuart during the morning break in the playground.

Bomber pushed open the classroom door and heads turned spontaneously towards the doorway. The momentary hush broke out into a frenzy of whispering as the boys filed into the classroom. Mr Barret was sat behind his desk in front of the chalk board, folded arms across his chest, and leaned back in his chair as each boy panted his apologies for being late. Mr Barret's steely blue eyes followed them as they sat behind two vacant double-flap-top desks, and he re-opened the registration book, pulled a pen from his top pocket and poised over the book ready to tick their attendance. He was a tough teacher and fair minded but if a pupil stepped out of line, he wouldn't hesitate to discipline the offender, in front of the whole class, with a few harsh strokes of his slipper. It was no coincidence that he was in charge of the 'rough' house in the school, and he demanded a valid reason for their lateness.

'Fire away,' said Mr Barret, expecting the usual mumbling of excuses.

Bomber held his hand up, glanced over at Porky sitting on the far side of the classroom next to the window, and began to explain. His explanation was however, lost in the whispering chatter of the class.

'Quiet!' Mr Barret shouted, and instant silence prevailed.

Mr Barret scanned the classroom with a scathing eye. 'Start again boy.'

'Well, sir—' said Bomber, and glanced over to Porky again.

'You can put your hand down now,' interrupted Mr Barret.

'The reason for us being late sir is… we found a First Year boy from Cook House who had been set upon. He was crying and in a right state. A gang of boys had thrown his books and lunch all over the shop, for no apparent reason. That was, sir, after they pulled him to the ground and searched him. He was in a proper mess, with chalk marks all over him, so we stopped and helped him.'

Porky slumped down behind his desk, his mind switched off in the belief that the rule of not snitching applied even more so under fear or threat, and he knew that the four boys were in fear.

'Did you find out the name of the boys responsible?' asked Mr Barret.

Porky was anxious at that point and confirmed his uneasiness by looking at the other three crew members in the class, and then flashed a glance at Bomber.

'Yes we did, sir,' replied Bomber, raising his tone of voice, and then pointed straight at Porky.

'It was him, sir. Porky and his gang, sir. Sir, Stuart, the boy who was set upon, will be informing Mr James, his Housemaster, this morning.'

At that moment the bell rang, signifying the end of registration and the start of the first period. Desktops banged and footwear scuffed on the floor as the class was mobilised into a mode of chatter, and moved towards the door.

'Sit down all of you,' shouted Mr Barret and glared at Porky.

The class returned to their desks.

'You, Smith,' said Mr Barret, calling Porky by his surname.

'Who, me sir?' Porky replied innocently.

'Yes *you* boy, is this true?' asked Mr Barret, expecting denial.

'No sir. Not like he says it was, sir. That boy is telling lies, sir.'

Mr Barret believed otherwise but without all those concerned in front of him, he was unable to assess the gravity of the incident. He decided to investigate the allegation properly with Mr James, before proceeding any further.

'Smith! You report back here after the last bell with those boys that were with you this morning, do you hear?' said Mr Barret.

'Yes sir,' replied Porky.

'Class dismissed.'

The class went on their way to the next lesson.

Porky was fuming and snaked his way toward Bomber, still seated at his desk. 'I'm going to do all four of you, you see if I don't,' he whispered, discreetly poking Bomber in his shoulder as he brushed past.

The next period was at the other end of the school, opposite the assembly hall, and the long corridor leading to the classes was busier than a tube station at rush hour. So, the boys hung back and allowed Porky plenty of time to get ahead while they sauntered together in the two way throng, discussing the likely outcome. Zip was under the impression that it would put a brake on all the brewing contention between the two groups, both in school and on the estate.

'You're kidding,' said Bomber.

'No, I'm not,' said Zip.

'I'll tell you what will happen—' said Bomber.

'I can guess,' interrupted Barley.' 'Porky will deny it to old man Barret. His cronies will back him up and it'll be Stuart's word against Porky and the gang.'

'Ah! What about us?' snapped Zip.

'We didn't turn up till afterwards, so we didn't witness Porky do a thing. He'll tell his cronies what to say; they'll all be in the picture by the time old man Barret talks to them. Old man Barret should have dealt with them there and then this morning,' said Barley.

'There's one good thing that's come out of all this,' said Danny, in a lighter mood.

'What's that then?' asked Bomber.

'While he's trying to get us, he's leaving everyone else alone.'

'What are we… punch bags for the whole school?' said Zip.

'He's got to catch us first,' said Bomber.

'Nuts to him anyway,' said Zip and pushed the classroom door open.

The teacher was chalking on the blackboard, with his back to the classroom. Porky and three of his crew had commandeered desks in the corner of the classroom, next to the window and overlooking the playground. Porky had also made sure the only seats available to the boys were just in front of him. With an eagle eye, he watched their every move as they entered the classroom and sat down.

'Zip,' whispered Porky, and leaned forward. 'I'm going to do all you grassers.'

Three crew members showed Zip a fist and then pointed to him.

'Not before I do you first, you plimsoll,' replied Zip.

Barley, Bomber and Danny were dumbfounded: this was totally out of character for Zip, for he never fired a word in anger. This time, they presumed he meant business.

'Good for you, Zip,' said Bomber. 'Don't let them grind us down. We're more than a match for those sacks of deadbrains.'

Porky seethed, and slammed his desk top in rage, as a warning of what to expect.

'Stop that noise,' the teacher shouted and turned to face the class. 'Pay attention all of you.' The lesson began.

Porky and crew had been rendered inactive during the morning break, and were powerless to intervene. As Stuart took advice from Bomber, at the other end of the playground, on how to keep clear of Porky, the latter could only watch from a distance and frown in scorn. Bomber knew Porky and crew would be waiting for them in the lunch break as they came out from the canteen, so the boys elected him to think up a short term plan that would outmanoeuvre their enemy.

Bomber's idea was first to bulldoze through the throng of boys in the corridor on the first bell at dinner time, run hell for leather across the playground between the prefabricated classrooms towards the canteen. Instead of lining up in the canteen for lunch, they would collect their bikes and peddle like mad out the school gates and head for home.

Bomber estimated that Porky would probably catch a glimpse of them running across the playground in the direction of the canteen, and assume they had stayed for lunch. After grabbing a bite to eat at home, they could stroll back to school unhindered, with the added reassurance that it would be safe after school, now that Porky and crew had an appointment with Mr Barret.

Bomber's strategy triumphed; they went home for lunch and sauntered back to school in plenty of time before the first period of the afternoon. They strolled past the first gate-entrance opposite the allotments and on to the next, past the boy's toilets and into the playground. Keeping their eyes peeled for Porky, they began weaving a path through the crowded playground towards the corridor entrance.

'It's surprising that Porky didn't keep a couple of look-outs on the gate,' said Zip amid the bustling din of boys.

'He did,' replied Bomber. 'He most probably thought that we would still be on our bikes. There's a good chance his zombies were behind the bike shed waiting for us. By the time he finds out we're on foot and comes through the other gate, he'll have missed his chance.'

'Hold up, hold up,' warned Danny, and came to a halt. 'Porky at three o'clock with dollops in tow.'

Porky came marching across the playground with his crew and in a pincher-like movement they encircled the boys, barring their way.

'I suppose you think you're smart?' said Porky, frustrated and angry.

'And clever,' said Zip. 'Don't forget just *how* clever we are.'

Danny, Bomber and Barley noted the crew surrounding them.

'Shut your mouth pea-brain,' said Bacon in a threatening tone.

'Who pulled your chain, lav-pan?' snarled Danny.

'I suppose you thought that was smart, blurting to old man Barret?' said Porky. 'Well, when I've finished with you, you won't be able to open your gob again.'

'We're going to give you a good kicking,' added Bacon and jostled Bomber from behind.

'You'll be black and blue. Think on that,' confirmed another crew member.

'You might get away from us today but there's always tomorrow and the next day. If not then, we'll get you lot in the summer holidays anyway,' threatened Porky.

'And if you go running home, who cares?' said Bacon, and the crew jeered.

Porky stepped forward and brandished his fist in a men-acing manner. 'Even if you did tell your mum or dad, what can they do? We haven't touched you yet. Mind you...' said Porky, as an afterthought. 'There *are* ways we could come to some arrangement.'

Confronted by an overpowering opposition and with threats of aggression, a creeping shroud of loathsome fear oppressed the boys' thoughts. They stood motionless, at a loss for words.

The duty teacher, Mr Jones, had spotted the boys squaring up to each other, and had come barging in between them. 'What's going on here?' he said and looked to Bomber for an explanation.

'Porky has been threatening us, sir,' said Bomber accus-ingly.

'Is this true, boy?' asked Mr Jones.

'Course not, sir,' replied Porky and grinned. 'We're only larking around sir, wasn't we?' he said to the crew.

'That's right, sir,' muttered the crew. 'No harm done, sir, just having a joke.'

Barley, Danny and Zip bolstered Bomber's claim by confirming his accusation but the crew continued to deny the threats and accused Barley and Danny of not telling the truth.

'I want you boys to stay down that end of the play-ground and you boys stay at the other end. Is that clear?' said Mr Jones.

Before any of the boys could respond to Mr Jones the bell rang and settled the issue.

'I'll be watching you,' said Mr Jones, intending the warning to apply to all the boys concerned. He took the view that it was healthy horse-play between boys and thought no more of it than that.

After the last afternoon period, Porky and crew stood in the corridor, while Mr James and Stuart were in the classroom with Mr Barret. Then, each crew member was questioned individually concerning the morning's events in the allotment. Each crew member gave the same version of events and strongly denied harassment of any kind.

Porky and crew's account of the incident was flawless. Too flawless for either teacher to believe however, and they suspected collusion. But, Mr Barret was left with no alternative than to give Porky and crew the benefit of the doubt. This was not without a caution and he informed them that behaviour of that sort would not be tolerated under any circumstances. He advised them that he would submit a formal report to the headmaster for the record.

Meanwhile, on the way home from school when the boys had reached Zip's house, they stopped and stood discussing the situation. They had put the brakes on Porky's aggression at school, just as well because it was the start of the summer holidays at the end of the following week. How were they going to stop Porky's marauding then?

'And what about the girl's dance on Saturday night?' said Danny.

The girl's annual dance promised to be the best night in the history of the school. Instead of the usual fuddy-duddy quartet, playing music for the waltz or the foxtrot, the girls had lined up a rock 'n roll band to play at the dance. There wasn't a boy in the school who wanted to miss that.

The boys decided to find a short term solution to im-mobilise Porky and his crew, at least till the following Monday, when they could re-assess the situation.

'I've got something that will fix Porky good and proper for the whole weekend,' blurted Zip, beaming with confidence.

Bomber give Zip a sideways glance of contempt.

'You, fix Porky?' the three other boys uttered in sur-prise.

'Why not? It's not unheard of. Look at David and Goliath: that was a choker for him,' said Zip, insistent that he could fix Porky.

'Tell us what it is then,' said Bomber, appeasing Zip with some interest.

They listened carefully to Zip's plan of action and liked what they heard, so astounded at his ingenuity that they readily agreed it was *the* strategy for Friday.

'Do they really work though, Zip?' asked Barley excitedly.

'Do they work! Two worked on me. Think what a packet will do? Just use your imagination,' chuckled Zip.

'Think Winners,' said Danny and clenched his fist.

'Well, that's the weekend taken care of. What about tomorrow? You know, the day *before* Friday!' said Bomber sarcastically.

Bomber thought, it was all very well devising plans to evade Porky and his crew, but a confrontation was inevitable. How to be the victor, not the vanquished, remained a dilemma in the back of his thoughts.

'I've got one up me sleeve for tomorrow,' said Barley. 'You can bet Porky and his crew will bring bikes to school; he knows we had the advantage over him today. Providing we can all be in early in the morning,' stressed Barley, 'my plan can't fail.'

'Oh yes,' said Danny, and looked straight at Barley. 'Some of us have to get out of bed very early in the mornings. You were going to help me this morning, remember.'

Barley's face reddened at his having forgotten his promise to help Danny collect eggs that morning. He'd stayed in bed.

'Did I say that?' fudged Barley. 'Are we going for my plan in the morning or what?'

'Might as well. Tell us about it,' said Bomber.

Chapter Five

The following morning, the boys made sure they were first to arrive at school so they could take their pick of parking racks in the bicycle shelter and they chose the racks nearest to the canteen entrance. Barley, Danny and Zip then headed back out of the school gates and over to the allotments where they lay in wait behind the hedgerow. Bomber stood guard at the gates to make sure he was able to entice Porky into the playground and leave the coast clear for the skulduggery they intended to inflict on the crew's bicycles. Barley's assumption had been correct: Porky and crew came cruising along Bell Lane on their bikes and headed straight towards Bomber. They peddled past the allotments and rode into school. When they found that all the bike racks were full, they left their bikes behind the prefab classrooms, out of view from the playground.

'Great,' mumbled Barley and chuckled with excited anticipation.

The three boys came out from hiding and crossed Bell Lane into school and headed straight for the crew's bicycles.

'Zip, you keep dicky-eye while we go to work,' said Barley.

Zip peeked round the corner of the prefab classrooms at the playground. 'All clear. No dirt bags in sight!'

Bomber made it appear obvious that he was waiting for the boys to come out of the toilets. Porky indeed assumed that that was the case and sauntered towards the toilets. As he did so, Bomber headed for the toilets and out of the other side, leading Porky up the garden path. Barley and Danny, the two would-be surgeons, selected the first bicycle and started to operate with a spanner.

'This one first,' said Barley, handling his patient roughly. 'Keep your eyes open, Zip.'

'Any bright spark seeing us messing with a bike would assume it was one of ours, anyway,' said Barley.

'What kid in his right mind would worry about the Pig's bike?' said Danny.

Luckily, the first bike had mud-guard lugs attached to the back of the front forks and was easy to doctor. Barley loosened the wheel nuts with a spanner, then tightened them by hand back into place.

'One down, five to go,' said Danny, and they moved onto the next bike.

On closer examination of the next bicycle, the mud-guard stabilisers were secured with the wheel nuts on either side of the forks.

'Drat,' said Barley and moved his attention on to the chain leading from the back wheel to the crank.

Barley located the split link, placed a thin screwdriver behind the sliding spring, and with a decisive push, bent the spring clasp off the link and threw it away. Danny held the bike chain at either side of the link as Barley pushed the link out.

'He won't be needing that,' said Barley and threw the link into the sports field.

Barley pulled a length of copper wire from his pocket and tied both ends of the chain together, thereby severely weakening the chain when put under pressure.

'Two down, four to go,' chuckled Danny and rested the bike against the wall.

'Champion,' remarked Barley and moved to the next patient.

By the time that all the bikes had been doctored, all that remained was to meet up with Bomber and clean the grease from their hands before going into class.

After registration, Mr Barret announced that tickets for the girl's dance would be sold that Friday afternoon at the end of the House meeting. He then warned that tickets could not be purchased at the door on Saturday night and looked straight at Porky when he said, 'Anyone without a ticket will not be admitted. Boys thinking of barging entry can forget it, as I and a member of staff from the girl's school will be on the door.' He then dismissed the class for the first period.

Porky and three of his crew lingered round the corner in the corridor, and waited for Bomber to come out of the classroom.

'Grass,' sneered Porky, as Bomber rounded the corner. 'Barret couldn't touch us, grassers.'

Both groups bunched up in the corridor and stood facing each other.

'I tell you what,' replied Bomber and squared up to Porky. 'I'd grass you up again, and again, for what you did to Stuart.'

'That's about your mark,' said Bacon.

'Shut up, lav-pan,' blurted Danny.

'You want to make something of it, damaged brain?' replied Bacon.

'If you like, fish-dip,' replied Danny.

'Whenever you want it,' added Porky and prodded his finger.

'This dinner time,' said Bomber. 'We'll sort you out over at the allotments.'

'Oh yeah?' sneered Porky. 'You lot better be there then.' Porky was brimming with confidence and thought the others had taken leave of their senses. 'You'll get more than a barney.'

'Likewise,' replied Bomber.

'I'll be there,' confirmed Porky.

'Make sure you are,' said Bomber flippantly.

'Don't worry. I will be,' warned Porky, then headed off down the corridor to the classroom, continually glancing back, over his shoulder at Bomber.

'That's him taken care of for today,' said Bomber and watched as Porky bounced down the corridor.

Chapter Six

The stale odour of the wooden hut, mingled with the aroma of cooked dinners being served at the far end of the canteen. The sunlight entered through small, square windows reflecting the feeble shine of the laminated dinner tables and bench seats squeaked and creaked with age to the applause of cutlery as pupils seated themselves down with full plates of food. Porky, sat at the end of his table with one leg on show, gulped his pudding down at record speed, then prompted his crew to hurry up. When the first sitting for lunch had finished, the duty teacher blew his whistle and the boys formed an orderly queue at the canteen entrance. Porky made sure that he filed in behind Bomber in the queue.

'Out of my way,' he growled. 'You're gonna suffer,' and barged Bomber to one side. He trundled down the steps and stood facing the entrance in wait for his crew to gather round.

Bomber stood staring at Porky and one by one Barley, Danny and Zip filtered out the canteen, and both gangs stood eyeing each other up. The word had spread in the playground during the morning break that a rumble between both gangs was happening over at the allotments, scheduled at dinner time. Hoards of pupils stood near the canteen steps, while others gathered at a safe distance in a big jostling circle, awaiting the outcome.

'You're gonna suffer,' repeated Porky and confirmed his threat with a nod of his head.

'You're right,' said Barley. 'Someone is going to suffer,' and glancing upwards, 'It's a nice day for it as well.'

'You better believe it, twit,' snarled Porky.

'Oh, I believe it all right,' replied Barley.

Bomber glanced over his shoulder at the canteen entrance and knew it was only a matter of time before the duty teacher would appear and put a stop to their game plan.

'Go and get your bikes, you dopes,' said Bomber. 'We'll see you over at the allotment and sort you out once and for all,' and with a large cheeky grin he stuck up two fingers for victory.

Porky almost snorted with rage at Bomber's gall. 'Come on, get your bikes,' he barked to his crew.

With the bicycles close at hand by the canteen entrance, the boys grabbed them and raced out of school over to the allotments. Bomber halted by a gap in the hedgerow, and chose a narrow dirt track that twisted across the centre of the allotments. With their bikes between their legs and the peddles cranked, ready for the off, the boys waited for Porky.

'Works every time,' chuckled Bomber.

'What does?' asked Zip.

'Winding Pig-features up, so that he doesn't think straight...' said Bomber and with an afterthought added, 'I hope you fixed their bikes good and proper, Barley.'

Barley's attention was fixed on the school gates and he calmly replied. 'So do I.'

'Aren't you sure?' asked Zip, panicking.

'As sure as Danny was about Porky going for a pleasant train ride,' replied Barley.

'*Now* he tells us,' chuckled Bomber.

Zip took note of the track he had to cycle across: it had plenty of ruts with half bricks and bits of concrete sticking up through the surface. He was convinced that it would provide a rough ride. That ought to do the trick, thought Zip and looked up at the school gates. 'Here they are.'

Porky and his crew came peddling like mad out of the school entrance, making a beeline for the boys. They were followed by hoards of pupils letting out American-Indian war cries, heading for the hedgerow, hoping to witness a big bundle.

'Don't forget,' said Barley. 'Let them get within thirty feet or so before we push off.'

'You'll be behind me then?' said Zip, and peddled off like a bat out of hell into the allotments.

Bomber then shouted 'Tossers', to Porky and his crew at the top of his voice.

'You stink like sewerage,' yelled Barley.

'You're all lav-pans that've never been flushed,' howled Danny.

After the trio had completed their narrative comments, they stood up on their peddles and peddled with all the might they could muster. In the frenzied acceleration the bicycles heaved from side to side, over humps and ruts, with a continuous plume of dust in their wake. The hoards of boys lining the hedgerow stood waving and cheering. Bomber trailed behind Danny and glanced over his shoulder. In a haze of dust he saw Porky hard on their heels, closely followed by his crew. Bomber turned back to see where he was steering to hear agonising screams of pain from behind him and the rapturous cheers of the boys standing by the hedgerow. That put a smile on his face. Two of the copper links inserted by Barley had snapped under the pressure and caused the bikers to slip down hard onto the crossbar. The boy behind Porky lifted the handlebars in an attempt to scale a bump, lost his front wheel and went down with an almighty crash. The two bicycles behind piled into him and the riders went hurtling over the handlebars to the ground. Increased shouting and applause from the spectators spurred Bomber on and he peddled faster. Porky, unaware of the crew's absence and was so intent on catching Bomber, that he thought the cheers were directed at his efforts. Bomber glanced over his shoulder again to see that Porky was still racing on like mad but caught a glimpse of Porky's crew writhing around in agony. Seeing two boys holding their scrotum urged Bomber to steer over every bump imaginable. When he saw a large deep rut in the track, he aimed straight for its centre, lifted the handlebars so that the front wheel cleared the rut and his bicycle landed with a heavy jolt but safely.

Porky likewise lifted his handlebars to clear the rut but his wheel fell off, the forks dug in the dirt, and he went flying over the top of the handlebars and landed flat on his face, amid a clattering chorus of bicycle steel.

Bomber heard Porky's cries of pain and halted. He viewed the scene from a safe distance and listened to the spectators cheer their praise, a bonus he had not expected, and it made him feel good about himself.

'Mission successful,' said Barley with a large grin.

'Porky was right,' said Zip. 'You're gonna suffer, from laughter more like!'

Porky was flat on the ground, nursing his wounds while his crew were more interested in examining their bicycles. Bomber cycled over to inspect the damage.

'You're a glutton for punishment, Porky Worky,' said Bomber.

Porky glared, about to say something, but Zip slipped in first. 'Get used to walking. It'll get rid of some of your weight.'

'You can laugh now,' groaned Porky. 'But you'll come unstuck once I've finished with you. You'll run out of luck and when you do, I'll be there waiting.'

'We've heard it all before,' said Bomber. 'Stick it up your bike pump and pump it.'

'Won't he ever learn?' said Barley and gazed at Porky nursing his wounds. 'You're a dumb-wit. Why don't you just accept it?'

With large grins on their faces, the boys cycled back towards the spectators lining the hedgerow, still yelling caustic jibes at Porky. Then Bomber raised his arm, clenched his fists and cycled into Bell Lane, and the throng of boys shouted his praise loud enough for Porky to hear.

Fearful of reprisals after school, the boys decided to leave their bicycles around the girls' side of the school and collect them after the last period. That's what they had decided to do the previous day but none of them had actually thought to make prior arrangements with any girl to facilitate that idea. Instead they had taken it for granted as a mere detail and had assumed the problem would solve itself. All except Bomber, who had realised that they couldn't just waltz into the girls' playground, uninvited, drop their bicycles wherever they wanted and just come back in and pick them up after school. The girls' school was strictly out of bounds and any boy found wandering where he shouldn't was dealt with in the harshest possible manner. Bomber *had* thought of that problem but wasn't very worried and had kept his notions to himself, knowing it was Barley who had the gift of the gab and he was content to push the ball into his court, when push came to shove. They cycled past the school gates, the main entrance, the car park and towards the girls' part of the school, laughing and joking at Porky's expense.

'By the way, Barley,' said Bomber out of the blue, winking at Danny and Zip, 'who you gonna have a word with?'

'What do you mean, a word?' replied Barley, in total surprise. 'What word? With whom? About what?'

'The bikes of course. We can't just go marching into the girls' playground like we owned the joint, or had you forgotten about that?' said Bomber, making sure all the votes went in his favour. 'That puts you square in the frame.'

'Why me?' said Barley.

'Margaret likes you,' said Danny, teasingly. 'She's always on the green, hoping her knight in shining armour will ride around the corner on his wheeled-horse.'

'I'll second that,' added Zip.

'Third it,' said Bomber.

'So, it's all settled then Barley. You're doing the chin-wagging,' said Danny.

They pulled up outside the girls' school and parked their bicycles against the iron railings. The green opposite had girls sprawled in clusters, chatting like penguins on a beach. Barley hadn't denied or confirmed their vote of confidence in his ability and was daunted at seeing so many girls looking at them and scrutinising them in every detail.

'Are you going to get chatting then?' Bomber said.

'I suppose so,' slurred Barley, reluctantly. Flummoxed, Barley stood with his hands in his pockets, gazing aimlessly, as though peering in a shop window unsure of the intended purchase.

Bomber, Danny and Zip went and stood up against the school railings and left Barley at the kerb side.

'What you hanging about for then, Barley?' said Danny.

'I'm looking for Margaret,' he replied, very flustered.

'You'll see her at the back,' whispered Bomber and smiled.

Margaret had seen the boys pull up and was watching with interest at their buffoonery: it was a rarity to see them round at the girls' side of the school, and she was to know the reason. Barley inevitably saw Margaret at the back of the green, and pointed at her, like a referee at a football match and beckoned to her, as if she deserved a booking. Margaret was in total disbelief at his clumsy attempts to attract her attention. 'Who does he think he is?' she declared and glanced away.

'It looks urgent, whatever it is he wants,' said one girl next to Margaret.

'Oh dear,' yawned Margaret. 'He's got problems then, as I'm sure as hell not moving from here.'

Danny went up to Barley and nudged him with his elbow. 'Go on. Go over there.'

'She should walk over and see what I want,' replied Barley.

Bomber was in disbelief. 'I don't believe you sometimes. It's us who need a favour, so it's up to you to do the running. That's why we voted on you.'

Barley was stubborn and wouldn't move away from the kerb, even though he looked rather conspicuous.

'Why don't you be truthful with us?' said Bomber. 'You like Margaret. You're just bashful 'cause there's loads of girls around and that's why your giving it the, "I'm in control" thing.'

'No I'm not,' denied Barley, and his cheeks reddened.

'Well, go on then,' said Zip, 'she'll think you're a right pancake.'

Barley's shy stubbornness wavered, and he darted across the road, and weaved his way in and out of the skirted pupils to the back of the green. He scratched his jowl and with a cherry face garbled, 'Margaret! Would you do us a favour?' Nervously, he glanced around over the sea of girls' heads and tried to give the appearance of being pressed for time.

'I beg your pardon? I didn't understand a word,' said Margaret, having heard exactly what he said.

Barley bent down on one knee so he would feel less obvious to his surroundings, and repeated his question in a whisper. 'Will you do us a favour?'

'I might, if you ask properly…' she replied in a whisper, then cautiously added in an equally hushed tone, 'providing it's not a hair-brained scheme of yours.'

'No, no. It's not a scheme,' said Barley. 'Nothing that will involve you anyway.'

'But it will involve me if I do you a favour,' replied Margaret.

Barley was tongue tied at her logical attitude and fell silent.

'Explain to me why you want a favour, what the favour is and I'll consider whether I'll help.'

Barley glanced round at the boys, signalled that he would be five more minutes, then briefly outlined to Margaret just why he needed a favour. Margaret listened encouragingly, with an agreeable nod of her head from time to time but remembered that Barley could be devious with his pranks. She had not forgotten the prank he'd pulled at her birthday party. He had found where her father kept his home-made wine, sneaked a couple of bottles from the shed and then replenished her guest's soft drinks with the turnip wine. Of course nobody realised until it was obvious, and her guests were steaming drunk. Children suddenly began falling about stupefied, puking all over the place; in the kitchen, the front room and even upstairs in her bedroom. That's how his nickname stuck, Barley as in barley wine.

Margaret was sympathetic and agreed to take care of the bicycles, provided they were at the gates on time after school. If Barley wanted help with the same arrangements the following morning, the same rule applied. 'Be on time Barley,' warned Margaret.

'We'll let you know after school, about tomorrow I mean,' said Barley.

'So long as you're not late though – my friends and I won't hang about waiting for you,' said Margaret.

Barley trundled back to the boys through the cluster of girls.

He reached the centre of the road and glanced back over his shoulder discreetly. Margaret waved and her lips curled up into a smile.

'Aah, that's touching,' said Bomber, mocking Barley. 'What a neat little wave.'

'On yer bike,' snapped Barley.

'I can't. Margaret's looking after my wheels,' grinned Bomber.

'Who said Margaret would look after the bikes?' he replied.

'That neat little wave she gave you or was it the look in her eyes – I'm not sure which,' jested Bomber.

'Come off it,' said Barley.

They trundled off and only to glance once back at their bicycles before rounding the corner.

'It's good of Maggot to help us out,' said Danny.

'We ought to stop calling her Maggot though,' said Barley, who was feeling remorseful. 'After all she's turned up trumps.'

'It's you that called her Maggot,' accused Zip.

'I know I did,' said Barley, 'but I reckon we ought to use her proper name now.'

'I want to give you some advice Barley,' said Bomber, nudging Danny and Zip. 'Don't get all your guests drunk at your wedding – Margaret wouldn't like that.'

Barley pushed Bomber into Danny and Zip. 'I'm not sending you lot invitations, you couldn't read real writing anyway!'

Chapter Seven

That Friday morning, Zip was sat on his bed with four packets of chewing gum; two packets of spearmint flavoured from the sweet shop and two packets from the pharmacy at the bottom of the avenue after school. Both packets were identical in size, shape and taste. The difference between them was that the two packets from the pharmacy were in fact laxatives. Zip carefully opened the triangular foil flaps of the ordinary spearmint gum and emptied the contents of both packets on top of his bedside cabinet. He kept the packaging intact and placed them to one side. Repeating the operation with the laxative chewing gum, he destroyed the packaging and then carefully replaced the laxative gum into the empty packaging of the regular gum.

'Great,' Zip muttered and admired his handy work. I defy anybody, thought Zip, who can taste the difference – except when they start working – then they'll know the difference all right. Zip chuckled to himself knowing Porky, who like any other bully... selfish and greedy, would be blighted by his own ignorant attitude and wouldn't suspect entrapment. Zip put the ordinary chewing gum tablets into the pocket of his trousers, shot out of the house to grab his bicycle and went to call for Bomber.

Chapter Eight

Margaret had kept her word and was waiting at the school gates, with two of her friends, ready to park the boys bicycles. Zip wasn't sure how long it would take the laxatives to work on Porky, and with this in mind suggested they make arrangements to collect their transport at dinner time. 'There's always a chance they may not have worked by then,' said Zip.

Margaret was amicable and assured them that she would be on the green for the duration of the lunch break, and could thus pop into the playground for the bicycles at any time.

When the boys rounded the corner and before they reached the gates by the boys' toilets, Zip shared out the regular chewing gum and they rehearsed a dummy run for approaching Porky in the playground. 'Can't fail,' said Zip. 'It's foolproof.'

'Hope you're right,' replied Bomber, chewing like mad.

'I've never been more right,' replied Zip with a glint in his eye.

They stood by the classrooms near the assembly hall, to scan the playground for Porky. They saw him. He was bouncing and barging his way through a throng of boys near the bicycle shed and halted by the prefab classrooms with his crew. They were tightly grouped and stood scouring the playground.

Zip glanced over at Porky, and then braced himself. 'Now's a good a time as any,' he said, and began to snake his way across the crowded playground towards his target. Zip was feeling nervous. If his ploy was to work, he couldn't afford to arouse Porky's suspicions in any way: he had to appear casual and pretend he was unaware of his quarry's presence. Zip glanced over his shoulder at Bomber just behind him, pulled out two packets of 'doctored' chewing gum from his pocket and held them in the palm of his hand. 'Do you boys want some more chewing gum?' said Zip, chewing his own gum for all he was worth.

Porky reached out and snatched the two packets of chewing gum from Zip's hand, leering back smugly.

'Yeah,' he sneered.

Zip halted in his tracks to act surprised at Porky's snatching of the gum.

'I didn't mean you,' said Zip and backed away.

Porky opened one of the packets, emptied the contents into his hand, shovelled the tablets of chewing gum into his mouth and handed the remaining to his crew. Staring straight at Zip, he chewed and chewed. 'What are you going to do about it?' he said, licking his lips.

'You can have them,' replied Zip, timidly.

'Too right I can,' snarled Porky. 'This is just the start of it. You lot have got problems, I can tell yer.'

Bomber, Barley and Danny's faces were blank, and they tried not to utter a word.

'I know,' said Zip. 'Will it be from laughing?'

'I've not finished yet,' warned Porky, pointing to Bomber.

Zip's expression was solemn, and he uttered meekly. 'That's for sure.'

'I'll be seeing you lot at dinner time,' Porky growled, threw the wrapper down onto the tarmac and headed off into the playground.

Barley, Bomber and Danny were under the impression that the laxative should have done its work by lunch time but in the duration of the morning periods, Porky didn't seem to suffer any ill effects at all, and his campaign of scowling glares continued behind the teacher's back.

Bomber was disappointed that Zip's plan hadn't shown any results, and they left Porky to stuff his face silly in the canteen.

At the last period in the afternoon before the house meeting, Porky still hadn't shown any effects from the chewing gum, and Bomber began to doubt the laxative's reliability. He even went as far as to say that Zip had grossly miscalculated the potency of the medicine. Zip on the other hand was positive, still guaranteeing the desired results. 'Fair enough,' he said. 'Perhaps it's taken longer than expected but boy when it does work, it's faster than a speeding bullet.'

Every Friday afternoon, at the House meeting, with over sixteen classrooms in the school equally divided among eight houses, high attendance was always guaranteed.

Most pupils thought the house meetings were the highlight of the week; a time when pupils could let off steam on any subject concerning the general running of the school. There were always complaints, suggestions, ideas, and with inter-house competitions always discussed, a raucous hour was assured. Senior boys took preference and always sat behind desks, while juniors stood lining the classroom walls, sitting on window ledges or anywhere they could cram their backsides. Barley, Bomber, Danny and Zip were among the last to bundle into the classroom, and they lined the wall facing Porky and three of his crew who were sat on the window ledge. Mr Barret, the house teachers, and the prefects all sat behind a desk in front of the sliding blackboard, where they listened to the secretary reading the minutes of the previous house meeting. When the secretary had finished, the senior boys raised questions on topical issues concerning the school, and the usual banter of the house meeting was soon under way.

Zip kept a discreet watch on Porky, willing the laxative to do its worst. Halfway into the house meeting, it looked like his earnest wish was about to be granted. Porky's face was ashen and both hands were clasped round his tummy. He was sat on the window ledge, his legs hanging over the radiator, with beads of perspiration oozing from his facial pores. He was fidgeting and was clearly facing a severe dilemma.

'You, Smith,' said Mr Barret, and the attention of the house turned to Porky. 'Keep still boy.'

'It's me tummy, sir,' said Porky, nursing his midriff. 'Agh sir,' he groaned. Porky soon realised that he was no longer in control of his muscles and broke wind. Liquid substance gushed from the bottom of his trouser legs and decorated the radiator.

'I can't stop meself,' he cried in a panic as another splurge of diarrhoea filled his trouser legs. Porky lifted one side of his backside to remove himself from the window ledge, slid off and splattered to the floor.

'He reeks!' shouted a senior boy nearby and within seconds, boys had cleared a space round Porky and packed themselves tighter than sardines in a tin can, away from Porky's sewerage.

The class was in uproar. The door and windows were flung open, and boys stood up on their desks, their fingers all pointing at Porky. 'He stinks, he smells, he stinks, he smells—'

'Order, order!' shouted Mr Barret, furious. 'Quiet!' he yelled and then he banged the top of the desk with a tremendous blow of his fist. 'Get down to the toilets, Smith,' frowned Mr Barret, the muscles of his jaw expanding and his teeth grinding.

Porky stood up and headed for the door.

The class of boys jostled and pushed back to make way for his exit. Porky then came to a halt in the doorway and looked back to Mr Barret. 'It's me tummy, sir,' he said and with both hands on his belly, he let go another large burst of flatulence!

Zip felt vindicated. His strategy had worked. He smothered his laughter. 'He's holding the wrong part!' he whispered to Bomber.

Mr Barret, still frowning with rage, sent a junior boy to fetch the caretaker.

Zip nudged Bomber and whispered from the corner of his mouth, 'Told you they worked.'

Bomber obscured his mouth with his hand and replied, 'Roll on the Bughutch tonight.'

Mr Barret filed the boys into the corridor, diverting attention by selling tickets for the girl's dance on Saturday night, cut the house meeting short and sent all the boys home early. Barley, Bomber, Danny and Zip sighed with relief, and looked forward to a trouble-free weekend without Porky.

Chapter Nine

The Premier Cinema, nicknamed the Bughutch by all the local kids, was the venue where every Friday night, kids would descend to relax and let off steam. It was their night out and the only time the house was full to capacity. Young couples sat smooching in the expensive seats at the back in complete bliss. The middle section of seats was engaged by patrons who had forgotten how to smooch, and who wanted to see a film that reminded them of how they had smooched as youngsters. The cheap seats at the front of the cinema housed kids, who not only went to watch the film but to have a noisy, rip-roaring time at the other patrons' expense.

Zip was ready with the mice. He divided them equally into little, pocket size bags. He had impressed on the boys that they should arrive early at the cinema, in order to choose prime seats and minimise their chances of being caught after the prank.

'We don't want to be barred for life,' said Zip, distributing the pouches of mice.

The once fine façade of the Premier picture palace was now weather beaten and in disrepair. The fluorescent lights on the canopy flickered, spent, above the entrance, and the worn treads of the black and white mosaic steps lacked lustre. The décor in the vestibule was dingy, and an overpowering perfume fragrance floated out from the cashier's kiosk when purchasing a ticket. Opening one of the four black, sticky doors, a strong musky smell from the gents wrestled with the nicotine from the usherette's cigarette dangling from her lips, as she smiled behind her veil of smoke and tore the tickets in half.

Retaining one half of the ticket, the embers on her cigarette glowed as she shone the torch's beam onto the patchwork of bubble gum littering the threadbare, burgundy carpet running down the aisle. The interior of the cinema was painted a pale, golden colour, the lights reflected a wispy glow and a blanket of hazy smoke swirled above the audience.

During the interlude before the main feature film, Zip had arranged to meet the others in the gents to set the time for his plan of action.

Zip and Danny were on one side of the cinema with Barley and Bomber on the other and exact timing was of the essence if they wanted maximum effect.

Zip and Danny trundled out of the gents to their seats and Barley and Bomber soon followed suit.

They whispered their intentions to all the boys sitting nearby and the word spread to every kid in the front seats, all ready to make a commotion, so that when the doorman came to investigate the trouble, he would be unable to apportion blame.

The lights began to fade, the music blared and the velvet curtains pleated to reveal the screen. After the trailers of forthcoming films and advertisements, the credits of the feature film flashed onto the screen, and the young kids erupted into rousing cheers of approval.

The audience began to slump back into their seats with glazed eyes. Young girls gripped boyfriend's arms, as though fighting against gravity and the boys fed the girl's faces to stabilise their positions. Grannies, dads and mums sat spellbound in the middle section, licking lollies and shoving sweet things into their mouths. At the back of the theatre, usherettes puffed like chimneys, the doorman stood in the vestibule reading his paper, the cashier counted cash, the manager put his feet up and had a cup of coffee in his office, and the projectionist read his book.

Close to ten o'clock, Zip, Danny, Bomber and Barley pulled the bagged field mice from their pockets simultaneously, slid off their seats, crouched down and let the seats spring back into place quietly. There they waited for the big hand to strike ten: in quick succession they lobbed their furry missiles, like hand grenades, over the heads of the audience into the area of courting couples. Even before they had lobbed the last mouse, screams from the back rows had already shattered the tranquil silence of the theatre.

'Sit down and shut up,' was one polite term. 'Go over the park if you want to do that,' came another remark, as hysterical screams reverberated from the back seats. Gradually, more and more abusive shouts echoed in the theatre.

'Shut her face can't you?' raged one man.

'You're all dippy,' ranted one woman and stood up to face the back seats. 'That's the young of today for you... they don't appreciate anything.'

All the kids in the front rows began to stamp their feet, cheered and then lobbed empty drink cartons over their heads at the audience. Screams rang out as the mice scampered indiscriminately, and the audience began vacating the seats in a mad rush for the exit doors. The doorman ran down the centre aisle. 'Don't panic, don't panic,' he pleaded but was pushed to the floor in the rush. Mass hysteria blossomed into pandemonium as patrons burst open the exit doors and young and old scrambled over the seats. The lights came on and the curtains pulled back across the screen. Meanwhile, the usherettes stood at the back and continued to puff merrily.

Zip and Danny jostled at the emergency exit, loving every minute. 'Didn't it empty quick?' said Danny, and his eyes sparkled in delight.

'That's because it was a horror show,' Zip replied and beamed with joy.

Bomber and Barley were among those first to stampede, and they made for an old bomb site opposite the cinema, where they concealed themselves behind bushes to view the plight of panicky patrons bundling out the exits. Crouching behind the bushes, they saw the doorman step out from the emergency exit and gaze in disbelief at the remnants of his fleeing audience. He scratched the back of his neck, and shook his head, stepped back inside and pulled the exit doors shut.

'I bet the manager has got something to say to him,' said a gleeful Barley.

'Yeah. Here's the bullet,' chuckled Bomber.

Zip and Danny were at the back of the exodus, mingled with a group of boys walking down Bell Lane. When the coast was clear they doubled back and met up with Barley and Bomber.

'Didn't it go well?' whispered Zip, creeping up next to Bomber.

'Ten out of ten for that one, Zip,' replied Bomber.

The lights on the canopy flickered out earlier than usual.

'Yes,' was the boys dampened cheer. They remained behind the bushy shadows to witness the usherettes trundle down the steps to go home, the doorman and the manager secure the main entrance and trundle away down the highroad.

'It's feed our face time. What do you reckon?' said Danny, and they told their episodes of the night's events.

They then made their way over to the fish 'n' chip shop and with a bag of chips and a saveloy soaked in salt 'n' vinegar, made their way home to make plans for replacing

Bob's eggs in his chicken shed. Danny reminded Barley of his track record for being an early bird: it wasn't impressive. If they were to bring their plan to a successful conclusion, they would have to be up early in the morning. 'The early bird catches the worm,' said Danny and persuaded Barley to sleep over at his house that night to guarantee his early rise.

Barley slept on the settee, covered by an old army blanket. With one leg hanging over the arm rest and the other displayed in the opposite direction on the carpet, he snored peacefully, his head under the blanket.

Danny was woken up by his instinctive internal alarm clock, peeled back the blankets and quietly dressed in the darkness. He then tiptoed over to the window and fingered the curtains back slightly to see the shadowy outline of the chicken shed at the bottom of Bob's garden. Just a few minutes dawn will break, thought Danny and crept down the stairs, into the living room. There he closed the door quickly and prevented Barley's snoring from travelling up the stairs. Danny stood over the settee looking down at his guest, who still hadn't stirred, so he shook him abruptly. 'Come on,' he whispered and pulled the blanket off Barley. 'We've got work to do.'

'Where? What's the time?' said Barley and threw his leg over the edge of the settee to make a pair again. He stretched and yawned, wiped his mouth with the back of his hand and palmed his hair flat. 'I'm thirsty,' he stated drearily, and reached for his trousers.

'We can grab a drink on the way out,' said Danny.

Barley fumbled his legs into his trousers, wedged his feet into his shoes, and headed in a trance-like state towards the kitchen. He slurped water from the cold tap, sprinkled his face and then both boys slipped silently out of the back door and headed down the garden path. Danny slid the box of eggs out from underneath the bench in his father's shed and opened the lid to show to Barley.

'More than I thought,' said Barley in surprise.

'Now to put them back without rousing the cockerel – that's an art in itself,' said Danny. He pulled up the bottom of the chain-link fence, wedged a lump of timber to hold it in place, then wriggled under the fence on his back.

Barley then passed the box of eggs through and slipped under the fence himself, into Bob's garden. Quietly and carefully, they opened the shed door and the cockerel let out a shallow crow. Danny brushed aside the straw, just inside the shed, and Barley handed the eggs to him one at a time until the eggs were heaped in a pyramid fashion.

'Bob can't miss them,' whispered Danny.

'He'd have to be blind,' replied Barley, more certain than ever that the scheme was going to pay dividends. The boys then crept back to Danny's house as stealthily as they had arrived but now that the artificial factors had been completed, they began to feel self doubt: how could they approach Bob without rousing his suspicions? They couldn't just go knocking on his front door, asking whether his chickens had left a pyramid of eggs in the shed? That wasn't exactly subtle, but on the other hand, they couldn't afford to leave it to Bob's discretion either, and miss their chance totally. There had to be a better way, and they decided upon showing a concerned, neighbourly attitude, casual in its appearance, yet subtle.

Barley's father worked for the River Lea Conservation Board. When river barges had seen better days they were taken out of commission and dismantled in a dry dock where he worked. Seizing the opportunity to reduce his household coal bill, Barley's father had purchased many Green Heart and Oak timbers to cut up for logs. Though the heavy timbers were cumbersome, they had been neatly stacked next to the shed at the bottom of his garden.

A special wooden horse for cutting the timbers, had also been built for they had proved extremely tough and would soon dull the sharpest of cross-cut saws. Barley and Danny thought that if they were busy cutting logs when Bob let his chickens out of the shed, he wouldn't suspect their motives, especially as they would be cutting logs for Barley's father.

Danny grasped the upright handle at one end of the saw, and the boys began pulling in a even rhythm. Within minutes, they were puffing and blowing like old windbags and the sweat was running down their faces. Even then, the log was only half cut: the mighty Oak was proving too much and they dropped to the ground exhausted.

'Phew!' said Danny. 'No wonder you run a mile when your old man says he's going to log on Sunday mornings.'

The morning sun was quite hot, the gruesome teeth of the saw reflected its glint and jogged their thoughts into action. They grasped the handles once more and half-heartedly tugged the saw until their arms ached like dead weights.

The log hit the ground with a dull thud, and the boys gasped for air like marathon runners. They were still unable to speak a word as Bob opened his back door and came out into the garden. Dragging his feet down the garden path, both thumbs typically hooked in waistcoat pocket, he halted and admired his growing vegetables. He then glanced up at the chicken shed, moved towards it a couple of steps, then looked back at the vegetables again.

'What's he doing?' panted Danny. 'Waiting for a train to come along, so he can shout "all aboard".'

'Shh... patience Danny,' puffed Barley. 'He'll hear you.'

'I'll *be* a patient if I have to keep cutting any more of these logs.'

Bob gazed up once more at the chicken shed, shuffled a couple more steps, then stood still.

'What's he doing? Shunting or what?' snarled Danny.

Bob shook his head side to side, turned and headed back to the house.

'I've had it,' said Danny, and jumped to his feet.

'Morning Bob,' he said, and sauntered over to the fence.

'Hello, young Danny,' replied Bob and trundled over to meet him.

'I've been watching you from the kitchen window. I wish I had all that raw energy – you're like spring chickens working out here this morning.'

'Talking of chickens, Bob, how're yours?' said Danny.

'I knew I'd forgotten something,' said Bob, with a sparkle in his eye. 'I've forgotten to let out the chickens.'

Bob uncorked a thumb from his waistcoat, and indicated to his house, 'Me wife's in the kitchen this very minute, pickling eggs.'

Joy and accomplishment swept over Barley and a smile curled his lips.

'I'm right,' said Barley, 'about the African chicken theory?'

Bob hooked his thumb back into his waistcoat pocket and looked at Barley in contempt. 'African chickens?' said Bob. 'That's a joke isn't it?'

'No, no, no, Bob,' said Barley, shaking his head vehemently. 'Didn't they leave a heap of eggs for you?'

'Heap of eggs?' laughed Bob.

'There *must* be a heap of eggs,' protested Danny.

'That's right,' confirmed Barley, 'there must be eggs.'

'Tell you what – I'll let the chickens out and I'll have a look,' said Bob.

He sauntered over to the chicken shed, let the chickens flutter out into the garden first and then checked inside. 'No eggs in here,' said Bob, 'unless that witch doctor you told me about, got wind of them and took 'em for 'is fry up.'

Barley's smile was wiped clean off his face and Danny was sickened.

'The old codger's having us over,' muttered Danny.

'African chickens,' mumbled Bob and threw his head back in fits of laughter. 'I'm glad I never went to school,' he chuckled. 'Least not your one,' and carried on laughing back up to his house.

Barley and Danny sat down and leant against the fence, utterly dejected.

Danny's head was in his hands but then he suddenly sprang to life.

'Tell you what,' he said with a determined expression on his face. 'It isn't over yet!'

'What do you mean?' asked Barley.

'When the girls' dance finishes tonight, we'll cosh two of 'em,' said Danny.

'Bob would never guess it was us, would he?' replied Barley sarcastically, dismissing the idea.

'Leave it to me!' said Danny. 'Let's go and get Bomber and Zip.'

Chapter Ten

Barley adjusted his attire in front of the mirror, ready for the dance and the last thing on his mind was two chickens. Wearing a charcoal grey two-piece suit with a white shirt and tie, he pranced up and down admiring his reflection. Glancing down at his blue suede shoes, he brushed them with his fingertips, posed sideways in the mirror. Satisfied with his frontal appearance, he glanced back over his shoulder, and then searched his face for blackheads.

Danny was wearing a black and white dog-tooth sports jacket, a pair of much prized blue jeans and a open neck white shirt. He put on his new baseball boots, levered his shirt collar over his jacket lapels and paraded back 'n' forth in front of the mantelpiece mirror.

Bomber, who had spent much time that afternoon cleaning his footwear in anticipation, broke his habit of being late and was waiting on time outside his front gate for the boys. He was dressed in a black plastic, vinyl-coated windcheater, a black shirt, black jeans and highly polished army boots.

Zip, dressed to be cool in the evening warmth, was wearing only a white shirt, light grey trousers and black crepe shoes.

Dancing and jigging on the way to the dance, each boy mimicked his favourite rock 'n' roll artist all the way down Bell Lane, until they heard the pounding of music emerging from the assembly hall. Danny pulled a comb from his inside pocket, and began grooving and grooming his hair to the sound of twanging guitars. Bomber mimicked him and then so did Barley. Zip, uninspired by their titillation, clicked his fingers to the distant beat of the music. 'I'd polish your boots as well, Bomber,' he chuckled.

'How does me hair look, Zip?' asked Bomber, stowing the comb in his back pocket.

'All right,' nodded Zip in approval.

'How does mine look?' asked Danny.

'And mine?' chirped Barley.

'All right. You all look the bizz,' replied Zip.

'Aren't you going to comb your hair, Zip?' asked Bomber.

Zip spread his hands and gently touched his hair. 'No need,' he said confidently.

'What are you wearing then?' enquired Bomber.

'My own brand of grease,' grinned Zip. 'I pinched some perfume from me mum and mixed it with some lard.'

'I've heard of hard up but never lard up!' retorted Danny.

'It works though,' said Zip. 'Who's gonna know?'

'I can see it, Zip,' said Bomber. 'You'll be sizzling to-night.'

They joined the queue alongside the assembly hall, their tickets at the ready. Mr James, a burly-looking teacher, was making his presence felt by walking up and down the queue, his arms folded menacingly across his chest. Mr Barret, accompanied by the Head Teacher from the girls' school, sat behind a desk just inside the doorway taking tickets. His austere expression was of indifference to the loud music, filtering from the assembly hall, and his eyes showed disbelief upon noting the style of dress of each pupil.

'Evening, Mr Barret,' said Bomber as he reached the head of the queue.

'Hello boy,' replied Mr Barret, and glanced straight at Bomber's boots. 'You can't come in here with those,' he said and pointed to them.

'Oh, sir,' said Bomber. 'Why not?'

'This is a dance not an assault course. You'll do some poor girl an injury.'

'He can't dance, sir,' piped Zip in Bomber's defence.

'What I can hear of it,' said Danny. 'That singer can't sing but he's up there. Is that an assault, sir?'

Boys and girls in the queue giggled and even Mr James smiled. Mr Barret's sharp glance, however, bored holes into Danny.

'He can always do a clog-dance, sir,' said Barley.

Mr Barret paused and Bomber awaited his decision. 'I'll let you in on one condition,' warned Mr Barret. 'When I've finished here, I'll bring you a pair of slippers and you can put *them* on.'

'No problem, sir,' replied Bomber.

'Meanwhile, no dancing,' said Mr Barret, and took Bomber's ticket.

'They're not the slippers you whack us with are they, sir?' chuckled Danny and handed over his ticket.

Mr Barret did not reply, and smiled.

Then the boys made their way along the corridor to the assembly hall and stood surveying the scene from the doorway. They watched the girls dancing with no inhibitions, showing the boys just why the dance was being held. Some boys gazed intently, others gaped and some leered but all applauded the girls' dancing by jogging their heads up and down. Barley conferred with the boys and they settled for seats near the stage. They then sat and convinced each other with vague excuses why they couldn't dance and listened to the band. For the best part of the evening, they creased their clobber in the chairs, only managing to animate themselves when nature called.

Bomber, like Danny and Zip, noticed Barley's discreet attempts to hide his interest in Margaret. When she was on the dance floor, he gazed sideways at her, and his eyes followed her to the refreshments bar. They also noted, the change on his face when she danced with a prefect. Bomber, more than the others remembered Barley in the juniors: he'd done everything to be noticed by Margaret – all but carry her books. He had wanted to sit next to her at her birthday party but was unable to as her cousin had sat there. His reaction had been to spike the kids' drinks. When Margaret hadn't chosen him for her team, they played outings, Barley was the one who had started shouting "Maggot" as they ran off. Then there was the time when they were making a camp over the allotments and Margaret was taking a shortcut home from swimming: he had gone running over to her, just to say hello. He's more than just keen, thought Bomber.

Towards the end of the evening, there wasn't much space left on the dance floor, and to show face most boys had plucked up enough courage to ask a girl to dance. Bomber gave a sideways nudge to Barley and urged him on. 'You gonna ask Margaret to dance then?' he said and winked to the boys to rally round.

'Go on – go over there and ask her,' said Zip.

'This next dance is the last,' said Danny. 'She can only say yes or no. If you don't ask, you'll never know.'

Barley sat mulling it over in his mind but didn't answer. The boys mumbled their criticism for his lack of response but then Barley stood up, buttoned his jacket, took a deep breath and marched across the dance floor to Margaret. Bomber's head dodged in all directions to catch glimpses of Barley dancing with Margaret in order to narrate any progress back to the boys.

Barley had got one hand on Margaret's shoulder, the other resting on her waist and both his arms were stretched out to the limit. She held him round the neck and was nodding her head to his chatter.

'What's the matter with him?' said Bomber. 'You could drive a bus between them.'

The last dance ended and Barley returned, with a bounce in his step and looking pleased with himself. He explained why. Margaret's friends lived in Freezywater, about a mile up the highroad. He was going to walk home with her across the allotments, so he had invited Margaret to walk along with them from the dance as far as the allotments.

Danny reminded Barley of their plan to cosh two chickens that night. 'We'll walk through estate to the other side of the allotments,' said Danny. 'We can meet you on the other side, as you walk back from Margaret's house.'

'I'll meet you by the lamp post then?' suggested Barley.

Bomber changed back into his army boots, returned the slippers to Mr Barret, and the five of them made their exit from the assembly hall.

Chapter Eleven

Porky had been made the laughing stock of the school and it was blatantly obvious to him who was to blame for his tummy problem. By Saturday morning when his bowel trauma had subsided, he was once more in the mood to teach his tormentors a lesson they wouldn't forget in a hurry. He thus hatched a scheming plan of revenge.

Although his crew had purchased tickets for the dance, it was no big deal dissuading them from towing the line, and persuading them to forfeit going to the dance on his orders. Hankering for a reprisal, Porky kept watch from his house for Bomber and the others strolling down Bell Lane on their way to the dance that evening, and made sure his scheme would come to fruition. Before the last dance had ended, Porky and crew concealed themselves behind the leafy hedgerow of the allotments, opposite the school gates, and watched the drips 'n' drabs of boys and girls stroll past. Porky had become anxious but his adrenaline fired his anger.

Upon hearing Bomber's familiar laughter and hobnailed boots scuffing the pavement Porky was put out and rattled too when Margaret stopped and chatted with the boys by the lamp post: he hadn't expected a girl to be in their company and she would wreck his whole plan. He pushed aside a leafy branch blighting his view and couldn't believe his luck: Margaret and Barley split up and were heading straight for the allotments. 'I couldn't have planned it better myself,' he mumbled to Bacon.

Porky had deviated from his original plan to surprise and sort out all four boys and decided to teach just Barley a lesson: a lesson that would demoralise the rest of his friends and render them easy prey for a later date. He lay in wait until his intended victim was only an outline in the darkness, then indicated his intentions for his crew to spread out and run, like creepy creatures of the night in pursuit of the unsuspecting quarry. 'Get him,' yelled Porky at the top of his voice, and screaming battle cries broke the silence of the night.

They pounced on Barley and brought him to the ground. Two crew members held Margaret at bay and before she had chance to protest they had muffled her mouth. While Margaret had an overwhelming tendency to struggle, she realised it was a revenge attack on Barley: provided she remained calm, no harm would befall her person. Barley kicked and struggled as three boys held him down. Porky stood over him, grinned and then grabbed his ankles and stood on them. 'You're gonna get done now, boy,' said Porky. 'You're gonna get some of your own medicine, that's for sure.' Porky kneeled on Barley's shins, leaned forward, swung a fist over his shoulder and hit Barley in the eye. 'Want another one do you?' he ranted and punched him in the mouth.

The crew urged Porky to strike another and a hammering blow was delivered to Barley's face. 'You want more?' laughed Porky. 'All right then, I'll let you have it.' He belted Barley in the cheek. Porky then stood up and with an almighty swing of his boot, kicked Barley's buttocks, for good measure.

'One down, three to go,' jeered Porky. 'Tell those other three grassers that it's their turn next.' With booming laughter the marauding crew ran off into the shadowy night, still shouting back insults. Margaret, incensed by such horrendous behaviour and seething at being held against her will, refused to let her emotions tinge her cool thinking and found it within herself to comfort Barley in his hour of need.

Chapter Twelve

Bomber, Danny and Zip were sitting under the lamp post and wondering what was keeping Barley for so long at Margaret's house.

'We should have been walking back by now to cosh two chickens,' said Danny.

'He can't be jabbering all this time,' replied Bomber, but then heard scuffing footsteps coming up from behind him.

'Where have you two been?' said Danny.

Barley stepped into the light nursing his wounds: he had a fat lip, a swollen cheek, a blackened eye and he looked a mess. 'Guess?' he said, pampering his swollen eye.

'Porky's work,' said Zip.

'Did they hurt you, Margaret?' enquired Danny.

Her anger was simmering now and she replied curtly, 'What do you think?' and stood there ticking like a time bomb.

Bomber inspected Barley's wounds. 'He's given you a right bashing. He belted you hard enough, didn't he?'

Danny and Zip zoomed in for a closer look, and Barley tilted his head obligingly. They turned and looked at each other and nodded in agreement. 'Nasty.'

Bomber, seeing Margaret's discomposure, suggested that they all walk her home for safety's sake.

Margaret listened to the boys talk amongst themselves about Porky's harassment. Bomber, an advocate of aggression, painted a clear picture of how to solve their problem. 'There's only one option left to us and that's to stand in front of him, smash a lump of timber over his nut and watch his face! As for the rest of his gang – without him they haven't the guts.'

'I don't reckon that,' piped Zip. 'Use your imagination. Creep up behind him and *then* smash him over the nut. You can always imagine what his face looks like.'

'Porky will pick us off one at a time, if we don't come up with a good idea. It's like he said, one down three to go,' grunted Barley.

Margaret couldn't believe her ears as the boys portrayed. Porky as unbeatable and she realised that not only were they out of stamina but that there was also no intelligible solution to their problem. 'Seems to me,' she said sharply, 'you're convincing yourselves that Porky is invincible. If you keep thinking that he *will* be, think positive.'

'We've tried doing things positive but they don't work,' replied Bomber. 'He's too determined.'

Barley dismissed Margaret's advice as out of hand, for she was a novice where boys' problems were concerned. 'You're a girl, Margaret,' he said. 'Us boys are different, if you get my meaning.'

Margaret came to a halt, and glared at Barley. 'Hold on.' Barley paid no notice and made it perfectly obvious that he wasn't about to listen to a girl's ideas. Margaret quickened her step, passed the boys then turned and faced them. 'Listen,' she said and made them halt. 'Different?' she said. 'I can outrun you, outswim you, I'm as strong as any of you, I perform gymnastics at school. I do things you lot only ever dream about. Oh yes I'm different all right.' She shook her head in disbelief. 'Now you've proved to me I can out-think you as well.' Margaret turned round in a huff and walked ahead swiftly while the boys followed behind like sheep.

'Margaret,' said Barley, 'I wasn't thinking.'

'That's just the trouble, Barley,' she said and gave him a piercing sideways glance, 'You were thinking but it's not good enough, is it?'

Barley apologised several times to Margaret but she was having none of it, and hastened her pace until she was home. She opened the front gate, turned round to face the boys, and gently secured the latch.

Bomber stepped forward. 'Margaret!' he said, 'How would you deal with the likes of Porky then?'

Margaret glanced down and thought for a moment. 'Off hand I don't know but he's no big deal.'

'Help us then, Margaret,' asked Bomber.

Margaret weighed up the situation: should she step over the boundaries of neutrality? On the other hand, she hadn't wanted to be involved in the boys' rivalry either but Porky had involved her the moment his crew grabbed her against her will. Having seen Porky's behaviour first hand meant that she could only compete if she played a game of subterfuge. She would bring about his downfall as a bully. 'What if I meet you tomorrow at the old gun-site around two o'clock?' said Margaret.

'You're on,' said Bomber.

Margaret didn't mention another word on the subject and left the boys by the gate to ponder, as she sauntered up the path to her front door.

Bob's chickens escaped Danny's plunder that night due to the fact that Barley was impressively beaten-up. 'It was a bad idea anyway,' said Danny. 'If Bob didn't believe the African chicken caper, he was hardly going to swallow a note scratched into the dirt by two chickens saying they'd run off to commit suicide!'

Chapter Thirteen

Bomber knocked on Barley's front door and rejoined Danny and Zip at the front gate. They had decided to allocate marks out of ten for the severity of Barley's injuries: no marks were awarded for a bruised cheek or fat lip. Only a black eye would be counted. Slowly the front door opened and out stepped the celebrity. Bomber's face beamed, Danny's masked outright laughter, and Zip tried to think of the appropriate words.

'Ten out of ten,' said Danny.

'Couldn't have done better myself,' said Bomber.

'Don't take any notice,' said Zip.

Barley grinned, pulled the door shut and sauntered towards the front gate.

'It could have been much worse,' said Zip.

'Worse?' said Barley, slamming the front gate behind him. 'What do you mean worse?'

'It could have been me,' laughed Zip.

They were all eager to know how Barley's parents had reacted to his injuries and fired a salvo of questions while they set off down the avenue. Barley had retained his mischievous glint even with a black eye, and he stretched the truth taller than the trees lining the avenue. The others listened and enjoyed his distorted spiel all the way to meeting Margaret.

The derelict gun-site was situated close to the railway station at the bottom of the avenue. The anti-aircraft gun had been mounted high up on a concrete plateau to protect the Royal Small Arms factory from bombing raids during the Second World War. The ammunition bunker storage was still accessible, though now void of live rounds. All that remained of the old defensive gun were the steep grassy banks leading up to the concrete plateau. Margaret was sitting on her bike at the bottom of the steep mound. She looked completely different than she'd done the previous night, now ruggedly dressed in jeans and a brown shirt. Margaret was astute, and saw the scepticism and self doubt in their faces. She knew what they must be thinking: what possible strategy could a *girl* devise to solve their problem? 'It's not a waste of time,' she said and dismounted her bicycle.

'No, course not,' denied Barley.

'Well, it's not,' she said sitting cross-legged on the grass.

'So, what have you got in mind?' said Bomber.

Margaret couldn't reveal her intentions at that point and it wasn't possible to draw any conclusions from the brief details Barley had mentioned on the green. If she was going to help them put a halt to Porky's harassment, she needed some answers and began with how the series of events had transpired. Her analytical probing was monotonous and bored the pants off the boys. Regardless of how they felt, she made her point and eventually her thinking time expanded into long silences. Finally, she outlined her ideas in a step by step programme for the oncoming week at school. In such detail, it sounded precise and she had even calculated Porky's reaction with such accuracy that it impressed the boys immensely.

'What do you think?' said Margaret at the four blank faces staring back at her.

'Yeah, yeah, you can't fail,' floundered Danny.

'Wrong, *we* can't fail.'

'Yeah,' said Zip, 'We can't fail.'

'Believe me, this plan won't backfire,' said Margaret, and stood up and grabbed her bicycle. 'You're all sure what to do?' she said. 'I'll meet you here on Tuesday evening for an update.'

'See you then,' they said simultaneously and watched her peddle out of the gun-site, bump down the kerb and ride out of sight.

'I'd like to know how she knows that Porky's gonna fall for it all,' said Zip.

'She's astutely cute, that's how!' replied Bomber.

Chapter Fourteen

Monday morning they rallied round at Zip's house, earlier than usual, with the intention of seeing first-hand just how Margaret was going to set the wheels of her plan in motion. They climbed over the garden fence, made their way along the railway embankment and nestled themselves behind the dwarf-wall encasing the bottom runner of the iron railings. From that vantage point they could get a clear view of both the terrace and the park. The sky was a clear blue as a result of the sun's hard work and pupils heading for school across the park, blurred into the shimmering haze. 'There she is,' chimed Bomber.

Margaret opened the front gate of Porky's house, and with a bounce in her stride trod up the garden path. She gave a confident rap on the knocker and upon hearing muffled barks of a dog, stepped back off the step. She also noticed the claw marks on the front door.

Margaret tossed her head back, let her silky hair loose across her shoulders and the sun glistened a blinding whiteness from her blouse. She made a minor adjustment to her ruby-red pencil skirt, then cast her blue-eyed gaze up at the front door.

The latch mechanism clicked and the door opened inwardly, with a reverberating crash on the passage wall. Porky stood on the doorstep, his arms folded across his chest. His eyes gorged her lithe, feminine figure from head to toe. 'What do you want?' he said abruptly.

'I called round to thank you, actually,' replied Margaret, politely.

'What for?' he asked, in total surprise. 'Because I belted up your boyfriend?' he laughed, placed both hands above him on the door frame and leaned heavily on one leg.

'I would have called round yesterday,' said Margaret, 'but I had prior arrangements.' She removed her satchel from her shoulder and placed it by her feet.

'So what's it you're thanking me for then?' said Porky and rubbed sleep from of his eyes.

'If it wasn't for you, Barley would still be bothering me,' said Margaret fingering the loose strands of hair from her face.

'Really?' replied Porky.

'Really,' said Margaret, reassuring him. 'It's true.'

Porky was mesmerised, overwhelmed by her feminine charm.

'Don't you believe me?' she purred and gazed tigerishly at Porky.

'He had it coming to him anyway,' he said and expanded his chest. 'I only wish I could have been at the dance – I would have made him look a total weed.'

Margaret picked up her satchel and placed the strap over her shoulder. 'Well thanks anyway.' With her smiling eyes fixed on Porky, she began walking backwards to the gate. 'See you then.'

'Yeah, yeah, er, let me grab my jacket and I'll walk to school with you,' he stammered.

Margaret lifted her brow and paused for a moment, '…I'd like that very much,' and smiled.

Two other crew members that lived on the far side of the park, had seen Porky with Margaret walking along the terrace, altered their course and headed straight to school. Barley supported his head with both hands under his chin and rolled over onto his side to face Bomber. 'Come Friday he won't know what's hit him. She found his Achilles heel all right.'

'Achilles heel?' said Danny. 'Who's he when he's at home.'

'That's Margaret's strategy,' confirmed Zip. 'It means find Porky's weakness.'

'We don't have to know all that,' chimed Bomber. 'As long as we do our part, that's good enough.'

With Margaret's strategy in mind they set off to school.

Mr Barret wanted to know how Barley had received his black eye and a simple excuse was supplied to deter further complications. With the usual glares, stares and jibes from the boys during registration the bell rang and the first period began. Porky was quick to put the record straight that he had sorted out Barley and with threatening overtones, informed Bomber he was next in line for the same treatment. Bomber expected some verbal abuse in the playground during the morning break but to his surprise it passed hassle-free. Porky was hanging around by the prefab classrooms preoccupied and didn't give the boys a second glance. Bomber decided that they should take advantage of the present lull in hostilities and prepare the groundwork for the plan on Friday night. Instead of waiting for lunch time, as Margaret had suggested, they began discreetly seeking out all the pupils that had been bullied by Porky.

Bomber and Barley, backed by Danny and Zip, convinced each individual boy that it was essential for them to take their part if they wanted to halt Porky's intimidation. But the boys were frightened and they needed persuasion and reassurance that there would be no reprisals from Porky. Bomber assured them of this, provided they were sworn to secrecy and the topic wasn't discussed in school or anywhere near Porky or his crew. If this was maintained, there would be no reprisals to worry about. Not one boy refused the chance to even the score with Porky and each pupil was able to point out another pupil who had been bullied at some time or other. There were so many boys brought to Bomber's attention that he realised that recruiting them all would take most of the week.

Porky wasn't worried about his crew or having lunch in the canteen at lunch time. When the bell rang, he barged his way through the corridor and made his way over to the park. He then spread his torso out on the grass and with both hands under his chin, he lingered with his thoughts and waited for Margaret to arrive. Margaret was purposely late for her meeting with Porky at lunch time but sauntered into the park, smiling as if filled with the joys of spring. She held her hand up and her fingers danced in acknowledgement. Porky's cheeks expanded with a grin, and he hurriedly heaved himself upright to sit cross-legged on the grass. Margaret calmly stated the obvious. 'I'm late.'

'Not much,' replied Porky and feasted his eyes upon her sleek figure as she sat down.

'Have you been waiting long?' smiled Margaret and with a constant gaze on Porky, she forked her fingers and brushed the hair back from her forehead.

'No, no, no.'

'Class was held back – Greek Mythology and all that,' she said. Margaret knew Porky was smitten by her attentions and used her lunch break to gain further insight into his flawed character. She recognised his thought patterns as anorexic. She realised too that beneath his bullyish ignorance there were some good qualities but they were hidden so deep in his personality that he would need considerable cultivation if they were to flower. However, that was time consuming and time was not available. She thus felt justified in playing a game of deception so initiated her next move and made arrangements with Porky to meet after school. Then she also suggested subsequent meetings for the coming week, with the single intention of separating Porky from his crew.

Porky was entranced by his new-found friendship. Having gone out with her in the evening, he could only think of Margaret in more familiar terms and couldn't wait to go out with her again. As the week passed, Porky and crew became more fragmented until they were in complete disarray, their intimidating presence in and around school considerably reduced.

On Friday at lunch, Margaret put the final touches to her plan and suggested they meet by the footbridge in the park that evening for a walk by the River Lea. 'It's quiet, with no one to bother us,' she said.

Porky was in a state of euphoria at her suggestion and jumped at the chance, suspecting nothing of Margaret's true motives.

The house meeting was held earlier that afternoon, due to the start of the summer holiday, and ended with Mr Barret shaking hands with every boy leaving school ready for adult life in the big wide world. Barley, Bomber, Danny and Zip hung back in the playground after the meeting to ensure that Porky had definitely gone home, before they made their way over to the allotments. When they arrived, there were over seventy boys waiting, each of whom had been intimidated by Porky at some time or other.

Bomber went and stood on the grassy knoll where they had found Stuart crying and beckoned all the boys to gather round. Before uttering another word, he checked every boy's face to make sure none of Porky's crew were present, then explained in precise detail the plan of action for later that night, so that every boy understood. 'Is that all clear?' he shouted.

'Yeah,' came an excited, unified reply.

Bomber then gave directions to the rendezvous point and the exact time every boy must be there. 'We'll teach Porky a lesson he'll not forget as long as he lives,' shouted Bomber and raised his arm with a clenched fist.

'Yeah,' was the booming reply.

Bomber paused and before disbanding the meeting, noted the unquestionable determination on each boy's face.' Tonight then,' he yelled.

'Tonight, tonight, tonight,' was the simultaneous response that erupted.

Barley, Bomber, Danny and Zip cut through the allotments to meet Margaret at the bottom of her road, confirmed all the arrangements were in place and waited, ready for that night.

Chapter Fifteen

Margaret put on her jeans and the evening being warm, slipped on only a T-shirt but as a precaution she threw a cardigan over her arm. She noted her reflection in the mirror at the top of the landing, trotted down the stairs and went out of the front door off to meet Porky.

She headed across the park diagonally from the allotments to the footbridge and halfway across the park, she could distinguish Porky leaning against the railings at the bottom of the steps. Margaret began to feel pangs of self reproach about the web of deception she had spun and even wondered whether to cancel the idea altogether. Was it a wrong doing? she asked herself, wrestling with her conscience. Or does the end justify the means? She wasn't sure but glanced up to see Porky waving and she acknowledged him. Upon nearing the footbridge, she noticed the shine on his shoes, they had been polished for the occasion. His trousers were pressed and he was wearing a clean shirt: she realised he'd made a real effort to impress her and felt sly at the part she was playing. 'Bet you thought I wasn't gonna show?' she said, sheepishly and stepped off the grass onto the flagstones.

'I knew you would,' he replied eyeing her up and down.

'Have you been waiting long?'

'Long enough,' he said, and they ascended the steps of the footbridge.

'I was standing in the middle of the bridge whilst I was waiting,' he said and halted in the centre of the gangway, gazing up the railway track towards the estate.

Margaret looked through the steel lattice railings. 'You can almost see the Brimsdown station from here,' she said.

'That isn't the only thing you can see,' he replied, gritting his teeth.

Margaret frowned, puzzled. 'What do you mean?'

'Those four clowns,' he snarled, with a venomous glare in his eyes. 'I saw them crossing the railway lines, I know what they're about, all right.'

Margaret continued peering through the railings, as a frightful, tingling chill rippled through her head to toe. 'What *are* they about?'

'Keeping out of my way,' he replied. 'The dummies don't think I'll go over the fields looking for them, but I will, now that the summer holidays are here.'

Margaret's feelings of guilt instantly dispersed and resolve was her main stay.

Porky had seen Bomber leading Barley, Danny and Zip over the railway lines from his house. They were heading for a single railway track that branched off from the main line. The single track weaved its way across open fields to the cut, the same cut that flowed along the back of the park, under the railway line by the footbridge and joined the River Lea downstream.

Bomber had made his way to the cut. The railway track bridging the cut on to the embankment overlooked a peninsula, a lonely secluded spot aptly nicknamed, 'the Jungle'. Overgrown bushes, shrubs and trees lined both sides of the railway embankment and formed a green, leafy tunnel from the cut, to the bridge crossing over the river. Although rarely used, it was tall enough for trains travelling on the railway track to and from the Royal Small Arms factory. When Bomber reached the halfway mark in the leafy tunnel, all the boys from the allotments were seated on either of the rusty railway lines. As he trod the railway sleepers between the lines, they all stood up and followed him in complete silence to the bridge crossing the river. Bomber glanced over his shoulder to all the boys behind and pointed to the top of the bridge. 'Is that high enough or what?' Every boy approved in total awe.

Bomber ambled halfway onto the bridge and cast his gaze back down between the gaps in the sleepers: the water rippled with the black shadows of woodland growing on the banks and reflected a malignant menace. A skylark twittered high above the Jungle as the water lapped the sheer banks of the river. Bomber glanced south. His eyes then followed the tow path to the river bending east, then north to the river bending west. Not a single person could be seen and the silence was lonely and eerie. He waved the 'all clear' and half of the boys trundled over the bridge to the other side, concealing themselves on either side of the embankment.

Bomber warded off the swirling mosquitoes around his face, then headed back to the boys waiting in the leafy green tunnel and beckoned them to gather round. 'You all know what's to be done... Spread out and hide,' he said softly.

Barley, Danny, Zip and all the boys nestled into the bushes on the embankment, cloaked by the leafy foliage.

Margaret and Porky had sauntered along the banks of the cut from the footbridge, scrambled up the embankment until they were overlooking the peninsula and stood looking down into the Jungle.

'Where we going? The Jungle?' said Porky, thinking he was at his journey's end.

'Just a bit further,' replied Margaret and coaxed him to tread the railway sleepers towards the river. When they reached the bridge, Margaret skipped a couple of sleepers onto the bridge. 'We're here,' she said and turned to face Porky.

Porky was puzzled and looked back at Margaret. 'I thought we were going—' but he stopped in utter surprise.

Suddenly, the bushes rustled and the embankment teamed with life as boys emerged from both sides and headed towards him. Porky was stunned.

'You've asked for this,' said Margaret, and all the boys encircled him. 'You've only got yourself to blame.'

Then the boys on the other side of the bridge came marching across. They were tightly grouped and blocked any escape route. Porky clapped eyes on Bomber. 'I might have known,' he said, his face pale. He trembled in fear at the seventy or more boys staring at him. 'What's all this?' he said, panicked.

Every single boy remained silent.

'You're about to find out,' replied Margaret.

'Find out what?' sneered Porky, mistaking the boys' silence for weakness.

'Grab him,' said Margaret.

The boys swarmed all over him until he was helpless and overpowered. They lifted him and passed him along on a tide of hands. Trampling bushes, they flattened the undergrowth as they manhandled him to the bottom of the embankment. There, they deposited him on the bottom of the forty-five degree steel capped girder of the bridge. The boys pulled his legs apart, lay him face down across the width of the girder, forced both his hands onto the steel rims on either side and he was then instructed to hold tight.

Bomber grasped a handful of Porky's hair and pulled his head back. 'Look up there,' he yelled in his ear. 'Go on look.'

The pack of boys started to chant. 'Up, up, up,' in a low tone, slowly increasing their volume. 'Up, up, up, up.'

'I can't. I can't,' Porky screamed and tears began streaming down his cheeks as he cried. 'I'm frightened.'

His cry went unheard in the din of chanting, 'Up, up, up, up.'

Bomber tightened his grip on Porky's hair, and yelled once more. 'Get up there or else we'll drown you. Can you hear them? They want blood... your blood.'

Sobbing and howling Porky clenched the steel rim with both hands, cuddled the width of the girder as if holding on to his mother's apron strings, and began to climb gingerly up the steel girder. 'I'm sorry. I'm sorry,' he sobbed as tears flowed. He realised it was retribution.

'Up, up, up, up, up,' ranted the pack of boys. They broke into laughter but began to chant again. 'Up, up, up, up.' The chanting was relentless.

Porky was horrified at the height and halted his ascent. Danny pulled out a catapult from his pocket and fired a shot below Porky's hands. A stinging crack sent a reverberating 'twang' through the steel girder and reminded Porky that he wasn't untouchable, even at that height. Margaret was standing at the back of the throng, watching Porky as he reached the apex of the steel girder at the top of the bridge.

'Crawl, crawl, crawl, crawl,' urged the throng.

Porky grappled along the girder, unable to look down, for on either side the drop was sheer into water or onto the track and he halted a third of the way across. Bomber, unsure of whether to pressurise Porky to crawl to the centre of the bridge, turned to Margaret for her opinion.

'Make him go all the way,' she said. 'He would if it was you. He'd make you do it all right.'

Danny fired a shot from his catapult and Bomber orchestrated the throng of boys to continue their chanting.

Porky crawled along, inch by inch, until he reached the centre of the bridge where he froze on the spot, as if welded to the girder.

Danny fired another stone and it whizzed close to Porky's head.

'That one was for luck,' said Danny and put his catapult in his pocket.

The chanting subsided and the crowd of boys stood looking up in silence.

'What now?' asked Barley.

'Leave him up there,' said Margaret. 'Let him stew.' She turned to look at Barley and shrugged her shoulders. 'Porky knows he's well and truly beaten.'

The camaraderie among the boys frittered and left Porky, with profound results.

Chapter Sixteen

'So what happened to Porky, Granddad?' asked Jessica.

'There are many bridges in life, Jessica. That was only the first bridge Porky encountered where Margaret was concerned,' I replied and smiled knowingly.

'I know, Granddad, but what happened to Porky?'

'Well, Porky remained on the bridge until it was dark and he was unable to see. The darkness gave him a false sense of security. He inched his way back down the bridge to the embankment and was safe. He was never seen again by Barley, Bomber, Danny or Zip or in school for that matter.'

Jessica had a questioning glint in her eyes and I could see her weighing up the situation.

'But Granddad, you said that was Porky's first bridge he had had encountered concerning Margaret?'

'That's true, Jessica. You see after that night Porky didn't venture out of his house for a whole two weeks and when he did, it was to go on holiday with his parents. On the way down to Hastings, they were involved in a horrific accident. Porky escaped with just a few cuts and bruises: if it hadn't been for him being stretched out behind the front seats of the van, it could have been much worse. Sadly, Porky's parents sustained horrendous injuries. Of course, Porky was never told how horrendous.

'Meanwhile, Porky went to live with his aunt and uncle at Freezywater (that's about two miles down the road from the terrace) whilst his parents recovered in hospital.

'Of course Porky's aunt knew from the outset how long her nephew would be staying and enlisted him with a school that was much nearer (mind you, his attitude had changed after that summer holiday) and believe it or not he never bullied another pupil.

'When Porky's parents had completely recovered he wanted to remain at his new school. His aunt and uncle were unable to have children, they cherished having Porky in the house and so things remained the same. Porky had a great time living with his parents at the weekends – he was spoilt in all manner of ways.

'Eventually when Porky left school for the adult life he was unable to settle down in a job he really enjoyed. The grass was always greener in the next field and he had this compelling urge to keep on the move in no particular direction.

'Then one night his aunt and uncle sat down with him, gave him some sound advice and pointed him in the right direction.

'Upon his next birthday Porky enlisted in the army (that was the best move he ever made) and he realised his true vocation. After serving about three years in the army Porky had returned home on leave. It was on a Saturday night, if I remember correctly... Porky had gone to Freezywater to visit his aunt and uncle. There was a dance on at St George's Church Hall. I'll never forget it... in full uniform Porky was... bold as brass he purchased a ticket at the door and waltzed straight onto the dance floor. That's where he met Margaret again and that lead to *the biggest* bridge of his life.'

'Well, what happened, Granddad?' asked Jessica impatiently.

I smiled and felt the very butterflies in my stomach as I had done as a young man and I replied, 'Porky married your Grandmother, I thank God.'